Every recipe in this book gives information on:

- the **number** of servings
- the **preparation time**, including cooking time
- the **nutritional value** per portion

The following symbols are used:

■	= simple
■ ■	= more complicated
■ ■ ■	= demanding

Kcal	= kilocalories (1 Kcal = 4.184 kJ)
P	= protein
F	= fat
C	= carbohydrate

NB	1g protein contains about 4 Kcal
	1g fat contains about 9 Kcal
	1g carbohydrate contains about 4 Kcal

Throughout the book all weights and measures are given first in metric, then in imperial measurements, for example: 100g/4oz and 600ml/1 pint

g	= gram
kg	= kilogram
ml	= millilitre
l	= litre
cm	= centimetre

oz	= ounce
fl oz	= fluid ounce
lb	= pound

| **tbsp** | = tablespoon (15ml) |
| **tsp** | = teaspoon (5ml) |

All temperatures are given in degrees Celsius and Fahrenheit and refer to the settings used on conventional electric ovens. The corresponding gas mark is also given.

175°–200°C/350°–400°F	**= Gas Mark 4–6**
200°–225°C/400°–450°F	**= Gas Mark 6–8**
225°–250°C/450°–475°F	**= Gas Mark 8–9**

- If you have a fan-assisted oven, the temperatures given should be reduced by 30°C/85°F.
- Times and settings for microwave ovens are given only in the section on Microwave Recipes.

CREATIVE
MEAT DISHES

RECIPES AND PHOTOGRAPHY

AN INTRODUCTION TO MEAT

– Friedrich W. Ehlert –
– Odette Teubner, Kerstin Mosny –

HEARTY HOME COOKING

– Rotraud Degner –
– Pete Eising –

DISHES FROM AROUND THE WORLD

– Rotraud Degner –
– Ulrich Kerth –

COOKING FOR SPECIAL OCCASIONS

– Marianne Kaltenbach –
– Rolf Feuz –

WHOLEFOOD RECIPES

– Doris Katharina Hessler –
– Ansgar Pudenz –

QUICK-AND-EASY RECIPES

– Cornelia Adam –
– Michael Brauner –

MICROWAVE RECIPES

– Monika Kellermann –
– Odette Teubner, Kerstin Mosny –

LEAN CUISINE

– Monika Kellermann –
– Anschlag & Goldmann –

Translated by UPS Translations, London
Edited by Josephine Bacon and Ros Cocks

CLB 4214
Published originally under the title
"Das Neue Menu: Fleisch"
by Mosaik Verlag GmbH, Munich
© Mosaik Verlag, Munich
Project co-ordinator: Peter Schmoeckel
Editors: Ulla Jacobs, Cornelia Klaeger, Heidrun Schaaf, Dr Renate Zeltner
Layout: Peter Pleischl, Paul Wollweber

This edition published in 1995 by Grange Books
an imprint of Grange Books PLC,
The Grange, Grange Yard, London, SE1 3AG
English translation copyright © 1995 by CLB Publishing, Godalming, Surrey
Typeset by Image Setting, Brighton, E. Sussex
Printed and Bound in Singapore
All rights reserved
ISBN 1-85627-761-5

CREATIVE
MEAT DISHES

Grange
BOOKS

Contents

Introduction to Meat

Despite a number of health scares, beef, veal, pork and lamb are as popular as ever. There is really no reason for anyone to exclude them from their diet, as good quality meat eaten in moderation, plays an important part in satisfying the body's needs. Although meat contains valuable protein, essential vitamins and minerals, it is not essential every day. How can you tell good quality meat, how do you cook it and – last but not least – which cut is best suited for which dish? The following introduction will provide all the information you need.

BEEF

Beef comes from oxen, heifers, bullocks, cows and bulls. Its quality depends on the sex and age of the animal, the type of feed and how well it has been reared. How a carcass is hung, the maturation process of the meat and the stresses suffered by the animal before slaughter are other important factors.

Cuts that are low in connective tissue, such as sirloin and fillet, are used mainly for frying and grilling and should always be well hung. While meat is hanging, lactic acid forms within the fibres and this helps to break down any connective tissue. In this way beef becomes more tender, more digestible and retains its flavour. Other cuts are also improved by hanging.

HALLMARKS OF QUALITY

Generally, beef should be deep red in colour, give off a pleasant smell and display a fine-fibred, marbled texture. Fresh beef should feel firm when handled. When cut, the flesh should glisten at the point of incision. If the surface of the cut is pressed lightly for a few seconds, no imprint should remain.

The beef in shops and supermarkets is generally from animals less than two years old. Meat from older animals is usually used in the production of sausages and other processed meats.

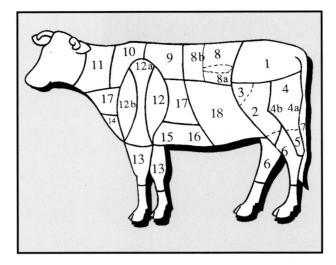

CUTS

Sirloin and fillet are the best cuts of beef, but many others provide very satisfying dishes, given the right cooking methods. Cuts that are low in connective tissue are not suited to boiling and braising, while a joint that is high in connective tissue is not suitable for roasting or frying, but is better boiled or braised. For tender, appetizing meat, the tougher tissues need moisture while cooking.

4a. Rolled topside
Steaks are cut from the rolled topside of young fattened beasts and are suitable for roasting, marinating and grilling.

4b. Top rump
This tender cut of beef can be sliced into steaks, but may also be boiled or casseroled. It is usually cooked in a stock.

 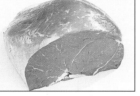

1. Rump
Steaks from the rump can be fried, but the joint is also suitable for roasting and braising.

3. Skirt
This cut is found inside the flank and may be used in goulash, ragoûts and other braised beef dishes.

5. Topside
A relatively tender cut with hardly any fatty tissue, topside is ideal in steak tartare and roulades, but can also be roasted.

2. Thick flank
Low in fat and connective tissue (gristle), this joint is ideal in roulades or steak tartare.

4. Shin, etc.
These hindquarters consist of shin, round, topside and silverside.

6. Leg
The flesh of the thigh yields good meat for soups and stocks.

7. Oxtail
Oxtail flesh is firm and gelatinous. The thicker end of the tail is best boiled in ragoûts, while the thinner end is used in soups.

9. Fore rib
Flesh from the fore rib is generally boiled, but it can also be grilled and roasted.

12a. Bladebone
This cut may be boiled or used in braised beef dishes. The layer of fat should be removed before cooking.

15. Brisket
Available fresh or salted, brisket should be boiled.

8. Sirloin
Sirloin joints are cut into various steaks including rump, minute and T-bone (4–6cm/ 1½-2½ inches thick, 600g– 1kg/1lb 6oz–2lbs).

10. Back rib
The succulent flesh is ideal for frying and for making goulashes and ragoûts.

12b. Thick rib
This cut resembles fillet in appearance, although the flesh is tougher. It is often used in thick soups, larded roasts and ragoûts.

16. Middle brisket
This part of the breast has fewer bones and is leaner than other breast cuts. The flesh is often used in soups.

8a. Fillet
Fillet of beef can be roasted whole or cut into portions. Steaks are cut from the thick end, while the middle is used for châteaubriand.

11. Neck
This cut may be casseroled in goulashes and ragoûts or roasted. If chopped, the meat is often added to hearty vegetable soups.

13. Shin
The meat from the lower leg is perfect for soups, but butchers often sell shin cut into slices with the marrowbone.

17. Thin rib
The animal's rib cage provides meat for boiling. The rib bones can be cut away from the boiled flesh.

8b. Prime rib
Butchers prepare cutlets, entrecôtes, double entrecôtes and joints for roasting from this part of the sirloin.

12. Leg-of-mutton cut
This superb cut of beef can be boiled or used in roulades and braised beef dishes.

14. Clod
Sold with the breast bones, clod is usually available untrimmed. It is suitable for boiling.

18. Flank
With bones or rolled without bones, flank is suitable for boiling and goulashes.

1. Rump
Rump is the most tender but also the most expensive cut from the top of the calf's leg and can be used as steaks, cutlets and escalopes.

2. Topside
This part of the leg is not quite so tender as the rump and is best served braised.

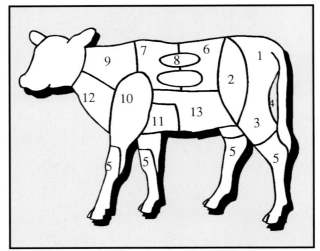

VEAL CUTS

Veal is a tender and easily digestible meat with a fine-fibred structure and no distinctive smell. Even the meat from fattened calves is low in fat and is usually covered by only a thin layer of white, fatty tissue.

The most highly regarded cuts are leg and loin. Rump, topside, thick flank and silverside from the leg provide veal escalopes. Veal is white to light pink and can be grilled, fried, stewed or braised.

10. Shoulder
Of comparable quality to the meat from the leg, shoulder can be roasted, boiled, braised, cut into steaks, strips or rolled.

11. Breast
A juicy, tasty meat which is often stuffed and roasted, but tastes just as good boiled, braised or rolled.

3. Thick flank
The thick flank provides excellent meat for steaks and escalopes. Use this joint for the classic Wiener Schnitzel.

5. Knuckle
Covered by sinewy tissues, the knuckle can be roasted whole or cut into slices.

8. Fillet
Veal medallions, the most tender and most popular veal cuts, are cut from the fillet, but it can also be roasted whole.

12. Scrag end of neck
If the fatty tissue is removed, scrag makes a lean cut which can be boiled or braised.

4. Silverside
The fibres on this cut are tougher than on the thick flank and make good roulades or a larded roast joint.

6.,7. Loin
Loin consists of two smaller cuts, (6) loin chops and (7) cutlets. The fillet and kidneys can be found underneath.

9. Neck
Although tasty and succulent, the meat contains bones, tissue and sinews.

13. Flank
Moist cooking is essential to make this thin cut tender and digestible.

PORK

Despite some concern over its possible health risks, pork remains very popular. This is because pork is economical, has a strong, succulent flavour and is usually the main constituent in sausages.

HALLMARKS OF QUALITY

The quality of pork has been the source of some discussion. One reason is that meat from factory-farmed pigs tends to shrink when fried, becoming tough and dry. For many years pig farmers have tried to please consumers, who tend to prefer less fat. It is certainly true that when reared in this way pigs are meatier, but the quality is much poorer.

Good quality pork should be permeated by fine streaks of fat, so that it stays tender and succulent when cooked. A thin layer of fat prevents the meat losing its juices and flavour. Surfaces should be moist and gleaming when cut. Unlike beef, pork does not need to be hung.

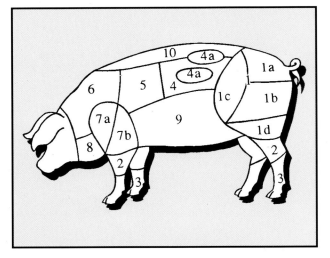

CUTS

There are numerous ways of cooking cuts of pork. Fried or grilled chops or cutlets are favourites for quick and simple dishes, but pork can just as easily be used in special recipes, such as peppered pork or glazed spare ribs. The addition of minced pork to a meatloaf creates a really juicy dish.

1a. Fillet end
This is the most tender part of the leg and is almost as good as fillet. It is suitable for frying as an escalope or a steak or roasting whole.

1. Leg
The leg is the firmest and meatiest part of the pig. The flesh is covered with a thin layer of fat which adds to the taste. Whether fresh, cured, smoked, roasted or boiled, leg of pork retains its flavour. The various raw and cooked meats derived from pork are usually made from the leg or thigh. The characteristic flavours of different types of hams vary from region to region, depending on the methods used for curing or smoking.

If a ham is cooked whole, the rind should be scored in a diamond pattern, so that the layer of fat immediately below can escape.

1b. Shank end
Most pork escalopes are cut across the fibres of this joint, but the tender meat from the middle leg can also be roasted whole. Cooked or smoked rolled hams are prepared from this section.

1c. Chump end
Most boiled hams come from this cut. Although many tendons permeate the flesh, it still fries well. Round end may also be roasted or boiled whole. Butchers will supply round end cured or uncured.

1d. Fore end
Usually sold as a joint for roasting or rolled with or without rind, fore end is a good choice for roulades and escalopes. It is also used for cooked and smoked hams.

4.,5.,6. Loin
Loin of pork consists of three sections, the saddle, i.e. the part with the short ribs, fillets and kidneys, rack of pork and the neck. The saddle and chops are sometimes known as the carré.

5. Rack of pork
Pork chops are usually cut from this joint, but it is sometimes cured whole, either raw or cooked, and then sold as smoked ribs. When combined with the saddle, it is used for cured rib of pork.

8. Breast
Pork breast is sold fresh or cured and can be roasted or boiled. Stuffed pork breast, ribs, goulash and various thick soups are some of the dishes prepared from this cut.

2. Knuckle
This is usually described as fore or hind knuckle. Whether fresh or cured, knuckle can be boiled or roasted. It is another cut which is prepared differently in various countries and regions.

4. Mid-loin
Mid-loin may be boiled, roasted, grilled, glazed or baked in pastry.

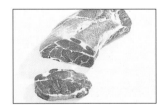

6. Neck end
This succulent cut streaked with fat and connective tissue is ideal for casseroles, roasts, goulash, ragoûts and pork strips. Spare ribs can be cooked whole or grilled in portions.

9. Belly
Sold fresh or cured, with or without bones, belly of pork can be stuffed, roasted or boiled, served warm or cold in aspic. Bacon is usually cured belly of pork and is sold smoked or unsmoked.

3. Trotter
Trotters are available fresh or cured and can be boiled, roasted, grilled or stuffed. They are sometimes used to enhance thick soups, sauces and stocks. In France trotters are served with truffles.

4a. Fillet (tenderloin)
Like most other types of meat, fillet of pork is the tenderest, juiciest and leanest meat. This fine cut is often roasted whole or in a crisp coating, such as puff pastry. It can also be prepared with vegetables or in a pork caul.

7a., 7b. Blade
The flesh from the shoulder is sold untrimmed with bones and rind and can be used for shoulder ham, ragoûts, goulash, blanquette, peppered pork and fricassées.
Lean meat can be used to make minced pork.

10. Back fat
Back fat is used for barding, larding and in pâtés.
It is available from many good-quality butchers salted, unsalted and smoked.

1. Leg of lamb
Almost invariably cooked whole with or without bones, it can be boiled, roasted, grilled and even occasionally cured. A large leg of lamb can be halved by cutting along the bone.

2. Loin of lamb
Loin of lamb is comprised of saddle, chop and best end of neck. The fillets and kidneys are found beneath the loin. The whole cut is sold untrimmed or halved lengthways to make loin chops, cutlets and medallions.

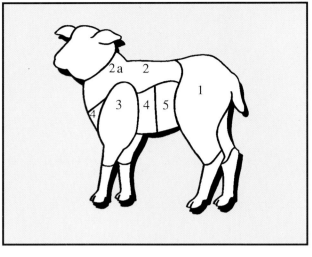

LAMB

Milk lamb, fattened lamb and spring lamb are the commonest sorts of lamb sold. As well as home-grown produce, frozen lamb is imported from New Zealand. This is high quality, as it matures in transit and reaches the British market at its best.

HALLMARKS OF QUALITY

Young lamb ranges from the light, white meat of the milk lamb (up to 6 weeks old) to the pink flesh of the fattened lamb (up to 12 months). Mutton, from older sheep, is dark red and coarse-fibred, but is no longer popular.
Well-hung lamb is deep red in colour and should be permeated with fine blood vessels and a thin coating of fat.

3. Shoulder of lamb
The meat from the shoulder is particularly tender and suitable not just for braising, but also for roasting and boiling. Shoulder joints are sold whole, rolled or cubed.

4. Breast of lamb
Lamb breast is a fatty joint with a good flavour. It requires long, slow, moist cooking and is, therefore, ideal for use in hearty soups. Breast of lamb can also be stuffed or rolled and then roasted.

CUTS

There are numerous ways to season or marinate lamb, and cooking methods include roasting, grilling and braising. The first step when preparing lamb is to pull off the parchment-like skin.

2a. Fillet of lamb
Lamb fillet is the most expensive part of the loin and ranks with fillet of beef and pork as one of the most highly regarded cuts. It is usually sold still attached to the loin chops. The best fillet comes from young lambs and will be well marbled with a fatty outer layer.

2b. Best end of neck
Cuts from the neck produce streaky, succulent meat that can be roasted, casseroled and boiled. It is suitable for moist cooking, such as hearty soups, lamb and bean stew, ragoûts or Irish Stew. Neck is available rolled or unrolled.

5. Flank
This fatty cut is the most economical of all lamb cuts. It requires moist cooking and is suitable for use in hearty soups. Boned and rolled, it is also often roasted.

THE CORRECT WAY TO PREPARE AND COOK MEAT

The tenderness of cooked meat depends not so much on the quality of the meat but on the method used to cook it. However, meat can be made more tender if it is first marinated, tenderized or pounded.

Cutlets, medallions, steaks, escalopes and roulades are usually pounded.

Meat consists of fibres which are linked together in bundles and then surrounded by connective tissue. Pounding with a steak hammer shortens the fibres and tears the strands of connective tissue, so that when the meat is fried it retains its juices. If meat is not pounded, when it is heated the connective tissues contract and the juices flow out leaving the meat both tough and dry. Pounding also produces a uniform thickness, so the slices cook evenly.

When preparing meat, such as steaks, cutlets and escalopes, for frying or grilling, it is important to slit any fatty tissues or gristle with a sharp knife, otherwise the surface will curl.

Tenderizing is a process sometimes used in professional kitchens and restaurants. The steak or escalope is passed through a tenderizer – a machine with two wheel cutters which break down the connective tissue. This gives the impression that the meat is tender, but actually, much of the juice is lost, reducing the cooking time by about a half. Like minced meat, tenderized meat must be eaten on the day of purchase.

Marinating. Steaks and other small cuts are often marinated, a process requiring a seasoned liquid, such as vinegar, wine, oil, butter or soured milk. The meat is left to soak in the liquid and the tannic and lactic acid bacteria loosen the connective tissues, the meat relaxes and becomes more tender. In addition, cooking times are reduced and the shelf life of the meat extended by four to five days. Frozen meat should not be marinated, as the cell structure is damaged by the freezing process and the meat juices are lost.

The marinade is often used in the preparation of the sauce.

Tenderizing agents, such as papain, have the effect of destroying protein enzymes. (Papain is found in papaya and pineapple.) Hundreds of years ago the natives of tropical countries noticed the meat-tenderizing properties of these fruits. Some chemically-produced tenderizing agents are now available, but no additives can replace the natural process of meat maturation.

Barding is used to protect tender meat from drying out and hardening around the outside.

Fresh, unsmoked pork back fat is required. This should be cut into thin strips, laid over the meat, usually in a lattice pattern, and then held in place with trussing thread. The fatty strips should be removed after roasting.

Larding is similar to barding. Pork fat is cut into 4–5cm/ 2–3-inch strips, then sewn into the outer surface of the meat joint with a trussing needle. About 3mm/⅛ inch of fat should be exposed at each end. Inevitably meat cells are damaged and so barding is preferable to larding.

Deep-frying in batter is a method suitable for raw or cooked offal, either sliced or whole. Some types of sliced meat are also suitable for this cooking method.

Meat for deep frying should be seasoned, dipped in batter and then fried at about 170°C/340°F. Wine or beer batters may be used for deep frying.

Coating with breadcrumbs is ideal not only for thin slices of meat or offal, but also for pieces of cooked meat coated in a sauce.

To coat an escalope, for example, season the meat with salt and pepper, dip first in flour, then in beaten egg and coat in breadcrumbs before frying.

Grated cheese, ground almonds or other nuts, herbs or desiccated coconut can be added to the breadcrumbs.

Roasting in the oven is advisable only for meats that are low in connective tissue, such as sirloin, fillet of beef, loin of veal, lamb or pork and some cuts from the leg or shoulder of lamb, pork or veal.

Relatively high cooking temperatures are required for this method. The joint is placed in hot fat and seared initially at 220–240°C/425–475°F/Gas Mark 7–9, and then finished at 150–200°C/300–400°F/ Gas Mark 2–6. Heat the roasting tin in a pre-heated oven or on the hob, add the fat and then the seasoned meat joint. After a few minutes turn the joint so that the hot fat seals all sides. Turn the meat frequently so that it browns all over.

As soon as it is well browned, lower the heat and continue to cook at the lower temperature. The juices should not be allowed to escape, as the meat will then braise rather than roast. It is a good idea to baste the joint with hot fat from time to time.

You can test whether a joint is cooked with a meat thermometer. The internal temperature of red meat, such as beef or lamb, should reach 55–65°C/100–120°F. For medium-roasted veal and pork, however, the meat thermometer should register 70–78°C/160–170°F. When the meat is cooked, leave it to rest on a cooling rack. Then, none of the valuable juices will be lost when it is carved and the process will also be easier.

Roasting with a fan-assisted oven. A fan circulates the hot air inside the oven which shortens cooking times. The oven temperature can be reduced and the joint roasts to a uniform brown.

Spit-roasting is a simple, straightforward and healthy way of cooking meat. It is suitable not just for joints, but also for whole animals, saddles and thighs. Fillets and sirloin may also be cooked on a rotisserie spit.

RARE, MEDIUM AND WELL DONE SIRLOIN STEAK

As sirloin is not a compact meat, it is impossible to give strict cooking times. Grilling or frying times depend not only on the weight, but also the thickness of the steak. A professional rule of thumb is that 1kg/2¼lbs meat requires 18–20 minutes.

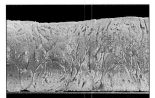

1. Rare steaks are red inside a thin layer of cooked meat.

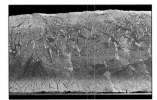

2. Medium steaks are a paler red.

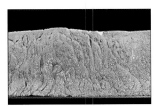

3. Well done steak is evenly cooked all through.

Quick-frying is suitable for chops, medallions, steaks, escalopes and strips. Meat and offal are usually cut into portions, seasoned to taste with salt and pepper and fried all over in hot oil or fat. When frying meat, it is generally advisable to ensure that it is turned over several times, so that the exposed side does not cool too quickly and the meat does not cook unevenly.

Good quality meat will not become tough if it is well seasoned before frying. Only meat of inferior quality meat, that has not been cooked properly or has matured insufficiently will produce an unsatisfying meal.

Grilling is a healthy, tasty and low-fat method of cooking meat. Cuts low in connective tissue are best suited to this method. Very little juice is lost, as the meat cooks quickly at very high temperatures (300–350°C/575–650°F) and is quickly sealed.

Make sure that you preheat the grill. Relatively thin slices of meat, such as escalopes, need be turned only once so that they do not dry out. Thicker steaks or chops, on the other hand, need to be turned twice, so that the characteristic lattice pattern is branded on the meat.

Make sure that the raw meat is salted and seasoned, brushed with oil and grilled at once. Finely chopped herbs and garlic may be added to the oil to give extra flavour. Neither meat nor offal should be pierced with a fork during grilling or frying. Instead, turn with a pair of tongs.

Steaming is mainly used for preparing light dishes. Little fat or liquid is required to cook food by this method, and veal which remains a pale colour is the obvious choice.

First melt a little butter or margarine in the top part of the steamer, add the seasoned meat and turn it once. As soon as the meat has lost its raw flesh colour, cover the saucepan adding a little water, if necessary.

For successful steaming, maintain a temperature of about 100°C/212°F within the covered steamer.

Braising consists first of searing meat to create the necessary colouring and flavour, and then completing the cooking by adding liquid to a dish that is then covered.

The ideal meat for braising comes from the thigh or shoulder and has a relatively high proportion of connective tissue. Whole joints, diced meat and knuckle slices are normally braised. The meat is often marinated before cooking, but should be well drained before browning. Season the meat and fry it all over in hot oil or fat. Fried vegetables, such as carrots and onions, and a little tomato purée may then be added. Return the water or the marinade to the dish, cover and simmer, stirring from time to time.

Braised topside of veal.

Blanching simply means immersing food first in boiling water and then plunging it straight into cold water or refreshing it under cold running water. Only a few types of offal need to be blanched.

Boiling is, strictly speaking, cooking in water or a stock at a temperature of 100°C/212°F. In fact, a slightly lower temperature of 85–95°C/185–200°F is preferable. The best cuts of meat for boiling are those with dense connective tissue, such as knuckle, breast, thigh or shoulder. Calf's head or offal, such as tongue and heart, can also be cooked in this way.

The golden rule has always been to make good stock add the meat to cold water, but to make good meat add it to hot water. However, research by food scientists has demonstrated the opposite. The constituents of a stock are the same, whether the meat is added hot or cold, but if meat for boiling is added to cold water, the meat enzymes will develop better.

As a rule, meat is boiled uncovered. Herbs and vegetables are usually added for the last 35 minutes of the cooking time, and can then be used to flavour sauces and gravies.

Meat should never be boiled for too long, otherwise it may become dry and stringy.

CUTTING VEAL

1. For recipes requiring thin strips of veal, first cut a piece of rump into 2cm/1-inch cubes and then slice thinly.

2. For veal ragoût, blanquette de veau or goulash, cut the meat into 4cm/1½-inch slices, then into strips about the same width and finally into cubes each weighing about 40g/1½oz.

GRILLING VEAL CUTLETS

1. Scrape the meat away from the rib tips.
2. Flatten each cutlet with a steak hammer. Pounding the meat shortens the fibres and tears the strands of connective tissue so the cutlet does not buckle during cooking.
3. Mix together dried herbs, such as sage, basil, thyme or oregano, and a little oil.

Season the cutlets with salt and pepper, and dip them in the herb oil.
4. Place the cutlets on a pre-heated grill pan.
5. Turn the cutlets over using tongs. If rotated a quarter of a turn, they will be branded with the characteristic lattice pattern.

1.

3.

2.

4.

5.

CARVING VEAL KNUCKLE

1. Hold a roasted knuckle of veal by the bone wrapped in a tea towel. Hold upright, and loosen the meat from the bone with a knife.

2. Use a fork to steady it, carve the veal into 1½cm/½-inch slices on a chopping board.

PREPARING CALF'S SWEETBREADS

1. Remove any fibres or blood vessels with a knife.

2. Leave the sweetbreads to soak in cold water for several hours, changing the water frequently.

3. When the sweetbreads are white and the water remains clear, drain and transfer to a pan of fresh, lightly salted water. Bring to the boil, and simmer for 3–4 minutes.

4. Plunge the sweetbreads into cold water and set aside to cool.

5. Return the sweetbreads to the pan, cover with cold water and cook according to the recipe.

6. When cooked, trim off any remaining skin and cut the sweetbreads into 5mm/¼-inch slices.

7. If the sweetbreads are required for a ragoût or a soup, each section must be carefully separated from the connecting tissue.

3.

4.

5.

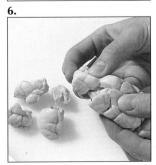

1.

6.

2.

7.

PREPARING CALF'S LIVER

1. Place the calf's liver in tepid water for 2–3 minutes.

2. If necessary, loosen the skin, push the thumb underneath and pull the skin off.

3. Starting at the thicker side, cut diagonally away from the flat side to make pencil-thick slices.

4. Sprinkle the liver slices with salt and pepper.

5. Dip the liver slices in flour and shake off any excess.

6. Melt a little butter in a frying pan, and gently fry the liver slices.

7. Use the prongs of a fork to turn the liver over two or three times until pink.

3.

4.

5.

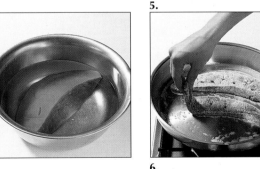

1.

6.

2.

7.

PREPARING PIG'S KIDNEYS

1. Remove the skin from the kidneys and lay them flat on a chopping board. Cut each kidney in half horizontally.

2. Use a knife with a sharp point to remove the white core from inside the kidney.

3. Rinse the kidneys thoroughly and pat dry. Pig's kidneys may also be blanched. To make 'Sour Kidneys', cut each halved kidney into 5mm/¼-inch slices.

PREPARING ROAST PORK WITH CRISP CRACKLING

1. Place a 1–1.2kg/2¼–2¾lb pork joint, rind downwards, in a large pan of cold water. To prevent the rind buckling, boil for a few minutes.

2. Use a sharp knife to cut a lattice pattern in the rind. These cuts allow the fat to escape during roasting. Rub salt into the flesh.

3. Cover the base of a roasting tin with water to a depth of 5mm/¼ inch. Place the pork joint in the tin, rind downwards. Add a few bones if available.

4. Sprinkle some caraway seeds over the meat, if liked, cover with a lid and roast in a preheated oven at 200°C/400°F/Gas Mark 6 for 25 minutes until sufficient fat has emerged.

5. Remove the lid and turn the joint over so that the rind is uppermost. Cook for a further 40–45 minutes, allowing the remaining water to evaporate.

6. From time to time, baste with fat and brush the rind with a little beer.

7. About 35 minutes before the end of the roasting time, add a peeled and diced onion and carrot.

8. Place the cooked joint on a cooling rack, pour off the fat and make a sauce with water or meat stock.

9. Mix together a little water and cornflour to make a smooth paste. Stir into the sauce to thicken. Strain and season to taste.

10. Cut the roast pork into slices and serve with the sauce.

1.

2.

3.

4.

5.

6.

7.

8.

9.

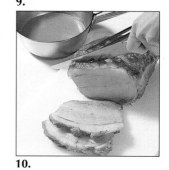

10.

Hearty Home Cooking

*S*unday lunch, the aroma of roast beef – home cooking's finest hour when delicious helpings of meat form the focal point for the family gathering. Yet it is the rich, tasty sauces that accompany roast beef, pork and veal that often prove to be the highlight.
Many of the recipes included in this section have been passed down through the generations, and it is here that their appeal lies. However, many new recipes have also been included, offering opportunities for serious home cooks to develop and extend their repertoires.

Spicy Meatloaf
(recipe page 28)

BEEF ROULADES

SERVES 4 ■
*Preparation and cooking
time: 1½ bours
Kcal per serving: 455
P = 36g, F = 30g, C = 5g*

4 x 150g–180g/5–6oz slices
   lean beef
salt
freshly ground black pepper
2 tbsps English mustard
4 thin slices streaky bacon,
   rinded
3 onions
2 small gherkins
4 rosemary sprigs
1 tbsp vegetable oil
15g/½oz butter
1 carrot
1 stick celery
2 tomatoes
10g/½oz dried mushrooms,
   soaked
½ bay leaf
4 black peppercorns
250ml/9 fl oz beef stock
125ml/4 fl oz red wine
4 tbsps crème fraîche

*Season the roulades, add the
filling and then roll up from the
narrow end.*

*Secure each roulade with a
cocktail stick or trussing thread.*

1. Press the slices of beef
with the flat edge of a
kitchen knife or with your
hands to flatten. Sprinkle
with pepper and coat with
mustard. Lay a slice of bacon
on top of each roulade.
2. Peel and chop the onions.
Quarter the gherkins lengthways. Finely chop or crush
the rosemary leaves. Divide
one third of the chopped
onion between the roulades.
Place 2 pieces of gherkin on
each roulade, sprinkle with
the rosemary and roll up
tightly from the narrow end.
Secure each roll with a trussing thread or a cocktail stick.
Heat the oil and butter in a
flameproof casserole, and
fry the roulades over a high
heat until browned on all
sides.
3. Peel the carrot and cut
into matchstick strips. Trim
the celery and cut into
matchstick strips. Blanch,
skin and chop the tomatoes.
Add the remaining onion,
carrot, celery and tomatoes
to the casserole, and cook
over a low heat for a further
5 minutes. Add the soaked
mushrooms, bay leaf and
peppercorns. Pour in the
wine and stock, cover and
braise for 1½ hours over a
low heat.
4. Remove the roulades.
Strain the cooking liquid and
rub it through a sieve or
purée in a blender. Return to
the pan, add the crème
fraîche, bring to the boil and
reduce slightly. Season to
taste with salt and pepper.
Return the roulades to the
sauce to reheat. Transfer to a
serving dish, remove the
cocktail sticks or trussing
thread and serve.
Serving suggestions: roast
potatoes and Brussels
sprouts.
Recommended drink: a
medium red wine.

SPICY MEATLOAF

(photograph page 26)

SERVES 4–6 ■
*Preparation and cooking
time: 1 bour
Kcal per serving if serving 4:
670
P = 38g, F = 45g, C = 29g*

100g/4oz gammon
400g/14oz minced beef
2 tbsps grated Gruyère cheese
¼ tsp cinnamon
2 eggs, lightly beaten
3 tbsps breadcrumbs, soaked
   in milk
juice of 1 lemon
salt
freshly ground black pepper
6 tbsps vegetable oil
4 tbsps breadcrumbs
1 onion
1 carrot
1 stick celery
4 tomatoes
6 tbsps cream

1. Finely chop the gammon
or finely mince in a food
processor. Mix together the
gammon, minced beef,
cheese, cinnamon, eggs,
breadcrumbs and lemon
juice, and season to taste
with salt and pepper. Knead
well to make a smooth mixture. Shape the mixture into
a loaf.
2. Heat the oil in a flameproof casserole. Dip the
meatloaf in the bread-
crumbs to coat. Fry the
meatloaf until browned all
over.
3. Peel and chop the onion
and carrot. Trim and slice
the celery. Add the onion,
carrot and celery to the
casserole, and fry for a further 5 minutes. Blanch, skin
and chop the tomatoes. Add
the tomatoes to the casserole, and season to taste
with salt and pepper.
4. Bake the meatloaf in a
preheated oven at 200°C/
400°F/Gas Mark 6 for about
30 minutes. Remove from
the dish and keep warm.

*Chop the gammon by hand or in
a food processor.*

*Fry the finely chopped vegetables
with the meatloaf before baking.*

5. Add 4 tbsps water to the
cooking juices, stir in the
cream and heat through.
Rub the sauce through a
sieve and serve separately.
Alternatively, retain the vegetables and pour the sauce
over the meatloaf.
Serving suggestions: boiled
potatoes with parsley and
assorted baby vegetables.
Recommended drinks:
chilled beer, apple juice or a
dry, white wine.

TIP

*Meatloaf can be
cooked in a
cooking brick,
but make sure
that it has been
soaked in water
first and do not
prebeat the oven.*

FILLET STEAK WITH ONIONS

SERVES 4 ■
*Preparation and cooking
time: 20 minutes
Marinate overnight
Kcal per serving: 610
P = 42g, F = 47g, C = 4g*

*4 x 200g/7oz fillet steaks
6 tbsps olive oil
4 onions
30g/1oz butter
salt
freshly ground black pepper*

1. Flatten the steaks slightly by pressing them with the heel of your hand. Place in a large, shallow dish and pour over 5 tbsps of the oil. Set aside to marinate overnight. Turn the steaks over from time to time.
2. Peel and slice the onions. Heat the remaining oil and the butter, and fry the onions until transparent. Remove from the pan and keep warm.
3. Drain the steaks and pat dry. Fry the steaks in the same pan for 4 minutes. Turn, season with salt and pepper and fry for a further 4 minutes. Remove from the pan and transfer to a warm serving dish. Top each steak with fried onions and serve immediately.
Serving suggestions: green beans tossed in butter, grilled tomatoes and buttered potatoes.
Recommended drinks: beer or a young, hearty red wine.

Pour 5 tbsps oil over the steaks and set aside to marinate.

Chop the onions and fry them in the butter and oil until transparent.

Fry the steaks in the onion-flavoured oil until browned on both sides.

PEPPERED STEAKS

SERVES 4 ■
*Preparation and cooking
time: 15-20 minutes
Kcal per serving: 360
P = 39g, F = 18g, C = 2g*

*4 x 200–250g/7–8oz fillet or
  sirloin steaks
2 tbsps coarsely crushed
  black peppercorns
1 tbsp oil
15g/½oz butter
salt
4 tsps brandy
2 shallots
125ml/4 fl oz beef stock
125ml/4 fl oz white wine
4 tbsps crème fraîche
2 tbsps cress*

1. Dry the steaks with kitchen paper and press the crushed peppercorns into the meat. Push down hard with the heel of your hand so that the pepper becomes embedded.
2. Heat the oil and butter in a frying pan, and fry the steaks for 3–4 minutes on each side until well browned. Warm the brandy in a small pan. Pour the brandy over the steaks, ignite and shake the pan until the flames die down. Remove the steaks from the pan and keep warm.
3. Peel and chop the shallots. Mix together the shallots, meat stock and wine, and bring to the boil in a small pan. Reduce to a third. Pour the stock and wine mixture into the frying pan, and scrape the base of the pan to deglaze. Beat in the crème fraîche over a medium heat until thick and creamy. Pour the sauce over the steaks and garnish with the cress.
Serving suggestions: mixed salad with French fries or crusty French bread.
Recommended drink: a medium red wine.

Press the crushed peppercorns firmly into the steaks.

Flambé the fried steaks with a little warmed brandy.

Deglaze the frying pan with wine and stock.

Add the crème fraîche and then reduce the sauce until it thickens, beating constantly.

VEAL ROULADES

SERVES 4 ■ ■

*Preparation and cooking
time: 1½ hours
Kcal per serving: 470
P = 42g, F = 29g, C = 5g*

*4 x 150g/5½oz long veal
    escalopes
salt
freshly ground black pepper
2 thin slices raw ham
1 tbsp vegetable oil
30g/1oz butter
1 onion
1 carrot
1 stick celery
fresh pork rind
3 sage leaves
125ml/4 fl oz white wine
125ml/4 fl oz beef stock*

FOR THE FILLING:
*15g/½oz butter
1 tbsp chopped shallots
100g/4oz mushrooms
150g/5½oz sausagemeat
1 tsp chopped fresh parsley
1 egg yolk
1 tbsp breadcrumbs
pinch dried thyme
salt
freshly ground black pepper*

*Blend the sausagemeat and
mushrooms in a food processor,
then add the parsley, egg yolk,
breadcrumbs and seasoning.*

*Place a slice of ham on each
escalope and spread the filling on
the top.*

1. Flatten the escalopes with
the heel of your hand. Rub in
a little salt and pepper.
2. To make the filling, melt
the butter and fry the shallots until transparent. Chop
the mushrooms. Place the
mushrooms and sausage-
meat in a food processor
and work briefly. Add the
parsley, egg yolk, bread-
crumbs, thyme and salt and
pepper and blend. Add the
sausagemeat mixture to the
shallots.
3. Cut the slices of ham in
half lengthways. Cover each
escalope with a strip of the
ham and spread the filling on
top. Roll up the escalopes
and secure with trussing
thread or cocktail sticks.
4. Heat the oil and half the
butter, and fry the roulades
until browned all over. Peel
and slice the onion and carrot. Trim the celery and cut
into matchstick strips. Add

the onion, carrot and celery
to the pan, and fry for a further 5 minutes. Add the pork
rind, sage, wine and stock,
cover, and cook for 45
minutes.
5. Transfer the roulades to a
serving dish and keep warm.
Drain the sauce and rub
through a sieve. Return to
the pan, bring to the boil and
allow to reduce a little. Stir in
the remaining butter. Pour
the sauce over the roulades
and serve immediately.
Serving suggestions: mashed potato and baby carrots.
Recommended drink: a
fruity white wine.

BRAISED KNUCKLE OF VEAL

SERVES 4 ■

*Preparation and cooking
time: 1¾ hours
Kcal per serving: 475
P = 83g, F = 11g, C = 5g*

*1 x 1.5kgs/3¼lbs knuckle of
    veal
salt
freshly ground white pepper
30g/1oz butter
250g/8oz belly of pork with
    rind
1 large onion
2 carrots
½ bay leaf
2 cloves
peel of 1 lemon
125ml/4 fl oz white wine
250ml/8 fl oz beef stock
2 tomatoes*

1. Wash the knuckle of veal
and pat dry. Rub in salt and
pepper. Melt the butter in a
flameproof casserole, and
fry the veal and belly of pork
until browned on all sides.
2. Peel and slice the onion
and carrots. Add the onions
and carrots to the casserole,
and fry for a further 5 minutes. Add the bay leaf,
cloves and lemon peel and
pour in the wine and stock.
Blanch, skin and chop the
tomatoes. Add the tomatoes
to the casserole, and season
to taste with salt and pepper.
3. Cover the casserole and
cook in a preheated oven at
200°C/400°F/Gas Mark 6
for 1¼ hours. Remove the lid
and return the casserole to
the oven for a further 15
minutes, basting the veal
with the liquid from time to
time.
4. Remove the veal and pork
from the casserole and keep
warm. If necessary, brown
the belly of pork in a hot
oven. Rub the cooking liquid through a sieve and pour
off the fat. Cut the veal into
slices. Remove the rind from
the pork and cut the meat

*Brown the veal and pork joints in
the melted butter.*

*Add the chopped carrots and
onion.*

*To make the gravy, rub the liquid
through a fine sieve.*

into slices. Arrange the veal
and pork together on a serving dish and hand the gravy
separately.
Serving suggestions: dumplings, peas and carrots.
Recommended drink: a
young, fruity white wine.

BRAISED CALVES' HEARTS

SERVES 4 ■
Preparation and cooking time:
30 minutes
Kcal per serving: 450
P = 29g, F = 28g, C = 4g

2 x 400g/14oz calves' hearts
salt
freshly ground white pepper
1 tbsp oil
15g/½oz butter

FOR THE SAUCE:
2-3 shallots
150g/5½oz fresh mushrooms
1 small carrot
1 stick celery
40g/1½oz butter
125ml/4 fl oz dry white wine
4 tbsps crème fraîche

1. Wash the calves' hearts and pat dry. Cut them in half and remove any skin, gristle and cartilage. Season well.
2. Heat the oil and butter in a frying pan, and fry the hearts until well browned all over. Cover and cook over a low heat for 10 minutes.
3. To make the sauce, peel and finely chop the shallots. Slice the mushrooms. Peel and chop the carrot. Trim and chop the celery.
4. Melt the butter in a small pan, and gently fry the shallots, mushrooms, carrot and celery for 10 minutes. Add the white wine, bring to the boil and allow to reduce slightly. Stir in the crème fraîche. Reduce the sauce again slightly.
5. Cut the heart into thin slices. They should still be a delicate pink inside. Arrange on a warm serving plate, and pour over the sauce.
You could substitute pigs' hearts (about 800g/1¾lbs).
Serving suggestions: noodles and salad.
Recommended drink: a medium white wine.

CALF'S LIVER WITH APPLES

SERVES 4 ■
Preparation and cooking time: 30 minutes
Kcal per serving: 385
P = 27g, F = 23g, C = 19g

4 x 125g/5oz slices calf's liver
2 large onions
2 tart apples
1 tbsp flour
salt
freshly ground black pepper
1 tbsp oil
40g/1½oz butter
4 thin rashers streaky bacon, rinded

1. Remove any skin and membranes from the liver. Starting at the thicker side, cut diagonally away from the flat side to make pencil-thick slices.
2. Peel and thinly slice the onions and push out into rings. Peel, core and slice the apples into rings. Season the flour with salt and pepper.
3. Heat the oil and 15g/½oz of the butter in a frying pan, and fry the bacon until crisp. Remove from the pan. Coat the liver with the seasoned flour, and fry for about 5 minutes turning once, until golden brown on both sides.
4. Melt the remaining butter in a second frying pan. Fry the apple slices until soft. Remove from the pan and keep warm. Fry the onion rings in the same pan.
5. Season the fried liver with pepper and arrange on a warm serving dish. Serve topped with the apple slices, onion rings and crisp bacon.
Serving suggestion: mashed potato.
Recommended drinks: cider or chilled beer.

Core the apples with an apple corer and then cut them into rings 1cm/½ inch thick.

Brown the liver on both sides.

Fry the apple slices in a separate frying pan until soft.

KIDNEYS WITH MUSTARD SAUCE

SERVES 4 ■
Preparation and cooking time: 30 minutes
Soaking time: 1 hour
Kcal per serving: 350
P = 22g, F = 27g, C = 3g

2 x 500g/1lb 2oz large calves' or lamb kidneys
salt
freshly ground black pepper
30g/1oz butter
1 small onion
150ml/5 fl oz crème fraîche
1 tbsp finely grated fresh root ginger
1 tbsp French or German mustard
2 tbsps snipped fresh chives

1. Core the kidneys and discard any membrane and skin. Place them in a bowl, cover with cold water and soak for 1 hour. Drain the kidneys, wash well and pat dry. Rub pepper into the flesh. Melt half the butter in a frying pan, and fry the kidneys all over for about 10 minutes. When all the liquid has evaporated season with salt.
2. Peel and chop the onion. Melt the remaining butter in a second pan, and gently fry the onion until transparent. Add the crème fraîche and ginger, and season lightly with salt. Allow to reduce slightly, stirring frequently.
3. Remove the kidneys from the pan and slice thinly. Transfer to a warm serving dish.
4. Pour the cooking juices into a small pan, and stir in the mustard and ginger cream. Heat through, and season to taste with salt and pepper.
5. Pour the hot sauce over the kidneys, sprinkle over the chives and serve.
Serving suggestions: mushrooms and roast potatoes.
Recommended drink: a full-bodied red wine.

HAM IN A LOAF

SERVES 6
*Preparation and cooking
time: 2½ hours
Soaking time: about 12 hours
Kcal per serving: 890
P = 62g, F = 38g, C = 75g*

1 x 1.5kgs/3¼lbs smoked leg
  of ham
1kg/2¼lbs bread dough
  (homemade or prepared
  from a ready-mix packet)
1 egg yolk
30g/1oz butter

*Roll out the dough to 1cm/½ inch
thick. Place rinded ham in the
centre of the dough.*

1. Place the ham in a deep
dish, cover with cold water
and set aside overnight to
soak.
2. Transfer the ham to a large
pan and cover with fresh
water. Bring to the boil and
simmer for 1 hour. Remove
the ham from the pan and
remove the rind.
3. Butter a roasting tin or
baking tray.

*Wrap the dough around the ham
so that none of the meat juices
can escape.*

4. Roll out the bread dough,
on a lightly floured surface,
to about 1cm/½ inch thick.
Place the ham in the centre
and carefully wrap the
dough around it to form a
secure parcel. Beat the egg
yolk with 1 tsp water and
brush the surface of the
dough with this glaze. Prick
the dough in several places
with a fork.

*Before baking, brush the dough
with a mixture of egg yolk and
water.*

5. Transfer the ham parcel to
the roasting tin or baking
tray. Bake in a preheated
oven at 190°C/375°F/Gas
Mark 5 for 1½ hours. Leave
to cool for 10 minutes before
cutting into thick slices.
Serving suggestion: horseradish sauce.
Recommended drink:
chilled beer.

> **TIP**
>
> *Any ham
> leftovers taste
> delicious with
> Cumberland
> sauce.*

PICKLED HAM KNUCKLE

SERVES 4
*Preparation and cooking
time: 2½ hours
Kcal per serving: 485
P = 29g, F = 42g, C = 0g*

1 x 1.5kgs/3¼lbs knuckle of
  ham
salt
1 large onion
1 bouquet garni
1 bay leaf
5 white peppercorns

1. Wash the ham in plenty of
cold salted water. Place in a
large pan, cover with water
and bring to the boil. Skim
off the froth. Peel and halve
the onion. Add the onion,
bouquet garni, bay leaf and
peppercorns to the pan.
Cook for 2–2½ hours over a
low heat. When the ham is
cooked it will come easily
away from the bone.
2. Remove the ham from the
pan and serve. The bone
may be very big and you
may prefer to remove it and
serve the ham cut into slices.
Serving suggestions: pease
pudding, cabbage and
mashed potatoes.
Recommended drinks: beer
or rosé wine.

> **TIP**
>
> *The knuckle can
> also be cooked
> on sauerkraut.
> Small, cured
> trotters also
> make an
> appetizing dish.*

LOIN OF PORK WITH CHERRY SAUCE

SERVES 4
*Preparation and cooking
time: 25 minutes
Kcal per serving: 415
P = 29g, F = 29g, C = 10g*

12 x 60g/2oz slices pork fillet
  or 4 x 150g/5½oz boned
  pork chops
salt
1 tsp ground ginger
1 tbsp vegetable oil
15g/½oz butter
6 tbsps canned Morello
  cherries, stoned
1 tbsp sugar
125ml/4 fl oz stock
4 tbsps crème fraîche

1. Rub the pork slices with a
little salt and a little ginger.
Heat the oil and butter, and
fry the meat on both sides
until well browned.
2. Drain the cherries and
reserve the juice. Fry the
cherries with the sugar in a
frying pan, stirring constantly, until the sugar begins to
caramelize.
3. Pour the stock into the
pan and bring to the boil.
Add the reserved cherry
juice, heat through and
allow to reduce slightly. Stir
in the crème fraîche and
reheat. Season with a little
ginger.
4. Arrange the meat on a
serving dish, and pour over a
little of the cherry sauce.
Serve the remaining sauce
separately.
This dish tastes marvellous if
fresh Morello cherries are
used.
Serving suggestion: potato
croquettes.
Recommended drink: medium dry white wine.

SPICY MEATBALLS

SERVES 4
Preparation and cooking time: 30 minutes
Kcal per serving: 370
P = 31g, F = 24g, C = 6g

1 onion
250g/8oz finely minced veal or beef
250g/8oz finely minced pork
3 tbsps flour or breadcrumbs
salt
freshly ground black pepper
1 egg
100ml/3 fl oz milk or mineral water
30g/1oz butter

1. Peel and finely chop or grate the onion. Mix together the onion, minced meat and the flour or breadcrumbs, and season to taste with salt and pepper. Add the egg and milk or mineral water to the meat and knead well until the mixture is light and easily workable.
2. Melt the butter in a frying pan. Use wet hands or 2 spoons dipped in water and make small meatballs. Shape them either into balls or flat burgers, and fry them over a low heat until golden brown all over.
Serving suggestions: potatoes, red cabbage or spinach.
Recommended drinks: beer or young red wine.

Add sufficient milk to the meat and flour or breadcrumbs to make a light, workable mixture.

Use 2 wet spoons to shape the meatballs, and to place them in the hot butter.

Fry the meatballs over a low heat until they are brown all over.

SPINACH ROLLS

SERVES 4
Preparation and cooking time: 50 minutes
Kcal per serving: 290
P = 14g, F = 22g, C = 8g

16 large spinach leaves
1 day-old bread roll or 2 thick slices white bread
1 onion
40g/1½ oz butter
1 tbsp chopped fresh parsley
250g/8oz sausagemeat
1 egg
pinch freshly grated nutmeg
125ml/4 fl oz stock
2 tbsps crème fraîche (optional)

1. Blanch each spinach leaf separately in boiling water for a few seconds. Spread the leaves out on a board. Tear the roll or bread into pieces, place in a bowl and cover with water. Set aside to soak. Peel and finely chop the onion. Melt 15g/½oz of the butter, and fry the onion and parsley for 5 minutes.
2. Squeeze the water from the roll or bread. Mix together the sausagemeat, roll or bread, egg and the onion and parsley mixture. Knead thoroughly and season with a little nutmeg. Place 2 spinach leaves together, spoon a little of the filling into the centre and roll up, keeping the leaf ends facing down. Repeat until the ingredients are used up.
3. Melt the remaining butter, and fry the spinach rolls all over. Add the stock, cover and simmer for 20–30 minutes. If liked, add the crème fraîche just before serving to thicken the sauce.
These spinach rolls make an excellent hors d'oeuvres served with crusty white bread.
Serving suggestion: mashed potato.
Recommended drink: a medium white wine.

PORK CHOPS WITH PAPRIKA SAUCE

SERVES 4
Preparation and cooking time: 15 minutes
Kcal per serving: 515
P = 26g, F = 41g, C = 10g

4 x 150g/5½oz pork chops
salt
2 tbsps flour
15g/½oz butter
1 tbsp oil
1 large onion
2 garlic cloves
2 tsps sweet paprika
2 tbsps tomato purée
200ml/7 fl oz crème fraîche

1. Rub the pork chops with a little salt, and dip in the flour. Heat the butter and oil in a frying pan, and fry the chops for 10 minutes, turning once, until golden brown. Remove from the pan and keep warm.
2. Peel and slice the onion. Peel and chop the garlic cloves. Fry the onion and garlic in the same pan for 5–7 minutes. Sprinkle over the paprika and stir in the tomato purée. Stir in the crème fraîche, and heat through. Return the chops to the pan and heat through for 2 minutes.
Serving suggestions: tagliatelle and cucumber salad.
Recommended drinks: beer or a red country wine.

> **TIP**
>
> *To make the paprika sauce a little hotter, add a small red chilli pepper to the onions, but remove before serving.*

Dishes from Around the World

*T*his chapter offers a selection of some of the best-known and most popular meat dishes from around the world, including specialities from French, Austrian and Italian cuisines, as well as exotic dishes from China, Turkey, the Middle East and India. Providing a wealth of ideas, this section is ideal for all adventurous cooks.

Cantonese Fondue
(recipe page 53)

41

BEEF WELLINGTON

SERVES 4 ■■

Preparation and cooking time: 1¼ hours
Kcal per serving: 870
P = 58g, F = 61g, C = 26g

1kg/2¼lbs fillet of beef
salt
freshly ground black pepper
60g/2oz butter
300g/10oz frozen puff pastry, thawed
1 egg yolk

FOR THE FILLING:
100g/4oz gammon
1 onion
150g/5½oz mushrooms
1 tbsp chopped fresh parsley
60g/2oz butter

Spread the filling in the middle of the rolled-out dough.

Place the fillet at one end of the filling so that it will surround the fillet when the pastry is folded.

1. Rinse the meat and pat dry. Rub a little salt and pepper into the flesh. Melt the butter in a roasting tin, and fry the beef fillet all over. Roast in a preheated oven at 250°C/475°F/Gas Mark 9 for 30 minutes, basting frequently. The fillet should remain red in the middle.
2. Lower oven temperature to 220°C/425°F/Gas Mark 7.
3. Meanwhile, make the filling. Dice the gammon. Peel and finely chop the onion. Finely chop the mushrooms. Melt the butter in a frying pan, and gently fry the gammon, onion, mushrooms and parsley for 5–7 minutes. Set aside to cool.
4. Roll out the pastry dough into a rectangle slightly longer than the fillet and three times as wide. Spread the cooled filling in the centre of the dough, place the beef on top and wrap the pastry around it. Roll up the open ends of the pastry sheet and press lightly to ensure that none of the meat juices escape. Beat the egg yolk and brush over the pastry dough. Decorate the top of the 'parcel' with pastry trimmings, if liked.

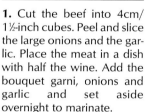

Decorate the top of the 'parcel' with strips of pastry and brush with egg yolk.

5. Rinse a baking tray in cold water and place the 'parcel' in the centre. Bake for 35 minutes until the pastry is golden brown. Serve warm or cold.
Serving suggestions: serve hot with mixed vegetables or cold with a salad or Cumberland sauce.
Recommended drink: a mature, fruity red wine.

BOEUF BOURGUIGNON

Burgundy beef

SERVES 6 ■■

Preparation and cooking time: 3–4 hours
Marinate overnight
Kcal per serving: 485
P = 39g, F = 18g, C = 9g

1kg/2¼lbs beef shoulder or rib
2 large onions
1 garlic clove
1 x 750 ml/26 fl oz bottle robust red wine
1 bouquet garni
100g/4oz bacon, rind removed
12 baby onions
1 tbsp sunflower oil
30g/1oz butter
2 carrots
salt
freshly ground black pepper
1 tbsp flour
250g/8oz mushrooms
4 tsps brandy

Set aside the meat and onions in red wine to marinate overnight.

Fry the bacon until the fat runs, add the baby onions and cook until golden brown.

1. Cut the beef into 4cm/1½-inch cubes. Peel and slice the large onions and the garlic. Place the meat in a dish with half the wine. Add the bouquet garni, onions and garlic and set aside overnight to marinate.
2. Chop the bacon. Peel the baby onions. Heat the oil and half the butter in a flameproof casserole, and fry the bacon until the fat runs. Add the baby onions, and stir-fry until golden. Remove the onions and bacon with a slotted spoon and set aside to drain.
3. Drain the meat and reserve the marinade. Pat dry and fry, stirring frequently, until lightly browned all over. Peel and dice the carrots, and fry for 5 minutes. Season to taste with salt and pepper, sprinkle over the flour and fry for a further 2–3 minutes. Sir in the reserved marinade and the remaining wine and heat through.

4. Cover and simmer for 3–3½ hours.
5. Wipe the mushrooms. Melt the remaining butter, and gently fry the mushrooms until all the liquid has evaporated. Add the mushrooms, baby onions and bacon to the casserole, and cook for a further 20 minutes over a low heat. Warm the brandy in a small pan. Pour over the meat, ignite and shake the pan until the flames die down.
Serving suggestions: boiled potatoes and garden peas.
Recommended drink: the same type of red wine that was used for the marinade.

BŒUF À LA MODE

Braised beef French style

SERVES 6 ■ ■
*Preparation and cooking
time: 5½ hours
Marinate overnight
Kcal per serving: 540
P = 43g, F = 28g, C = 13g*

*1 x 1kg/2¼lbs rump or
topside of beef
100g/4oz streaky bacon, rind
removed
4 tsps brandy
salt
freshly ground black pepper
pinch ground ginger
pinch freshly grated nutmeg
500ml/18 fl oz dry white
wine
1 bouquet garni
1 calf's foot
1 piece pork rind
1 large carrot
60g/2oz butter or lard
1 onion, peeled and studded
with 3 cloves
250ml/8 fl oz beef stock*

TO SERVE:
*500g/1lb 2oz carrots
16 baby onions
30g/1oz butter*

1. Rinse the beef and pat dry. Cut the bacon into strips, dip them in 2 tablespoons of brandy, sprinkle with pepper, ginger and nutmeg and set aside for 30 minutes.
2. Lard the meat with the bacon strips, inserting them in the same direction as the meat fibres. Rub salt and pepper into the flesh. Place the meat in a small dish and pour over the wine and the remaining brandy, add the bouquet garni and set aside overnight to marinate.
3. Place the calf's foot and pork rind in a large pan, cover with cold water and bring to the boil. Remove from the heat and set aside to cool.
4. Peel the carrot. Melt the butter or lard in a heavy,

flameproof casserole. Drain the beef and pat dry. Fry the beef until browned all over. Add the calf's foot, pork rind, carrot and onion, and fry for 10 minutes. Pour in the marinade and stock and cover.
5. Simmer the beef for 4 hours over a low heat or cook in a preheated oven at 200°C/400°F/Gas Mark 6 for 4 hours.
6. To prepare the dish for serving, peel and thickly slice the carrots. Peel the onions. Melt the butter, and gently fry the onions and carrots until golden.
7. Remove the meat, calf's foot and pork rind from the dish. Dice the calf's foot and pork rind. Rub the sauce through a sieve. (The vegetables in the sauce will help to bind it.) If the sauce is too thick, add a glass of wine. Season to taste with salt. Return the meat, sliced carrots, sauce, chopped calf's foot and pork rind to the dish. Cover and cook gently for a further hour.
8. Remove the meat and set aside to stand, then cut into slices. Skim any fat from the sauce, and season again if required. Arrange the meat slices on a warm serving dish, pour over the sauce and garnish with the vegetables and pork rind. Alternatively, carve the beef at the table.
Serving suggestion: baked potatoes.
Recommended drink: the same type of wine that was used for the marinade.

ROAST BEEF AND YORKSHIRE PUDDING

SERVES 6–8 ■ ■
*Preparation and cooking
time: about 2 hours
Kcal per serving if serving 6:
480
P = 40g, F = 29g, C = 16g*

*1 x 1–1.5kgs/2¼–3¼lbs sirloin
of beef
60g/2oz butter
salt
freshly ground black pepper
125ml/4 fl oz beef stock or
wine*

**FOR THE YORKSHIRE
PUDDING:**
*2 eggs
125g/5oz flour
½ tsp salt
250ml/8 fl oz milk
30g/1oz lard or dripping*

1. Rinse the sirloin and pat dry. Melt the butter and brush over the meat. Sprinkle with pepper. Place the meat in a large roasting tin and roast in a preheated oven at 220°C/425°F/Gas Mark 7 for 15 minutes. Lower the temperature to 190°C/375°F/Gas Mark 5. Season the meat with salt, and pour the stock or wine into the roasting tin.
2. Roast the beef as follows: allow 18 minutes per 500g/1lb for rare beef, 22–25 minutes per 500g/1lb for medium, and 30 minutes per 500g/1lb for well done.
3. To make the Yorkshire pudding, beat the eggs. Sift the flour and salt into a bowl and make a well in the centre. Gradually beat in the eggs and 125ml/4 fl oz of the milk. Add the remaining milk and beat to form a smooth, thin batter. Cover and leave to stand in a cool place for 1 hour.
4. About 30 minutes before the beef is ready, melt the lard or dripping in a large

Before roasting, brush melted butter over the beef joint and sprinkle generously with pepper.

rectangular roasting tin or a Yorkshire pudding tray or patty tins for individual portions. Beat the batter and pour into the tray. Place on the top shelf of the oven and cook for 25 minutes until well-risen and golden brown.
5. Remove the meat from the oven and set aside on a warm dish to stand for 15 minutes. To make the gravy, combine the meat juices with a little water and heat through. Cut the Yorkshire pudding into portions with a sharp knife or remove the individual puddings from the tray and serve with the beef.
Serving suggestion: garden peas.

Recommended drink: a mature red wine.

BEEF STROGANOFF

SERVES 4 ■

Preparation and cooking time: 30 minutes
Kcal per serving: 355
P = 26g, F = 26g, C = 3g

500g/1lb 2oz fillet of beef
3 tbsps sunflower oil
2 small onions
150g/5½oz mushrooms
15g/½oz butter
3 tbsps white wine
1 gherkin
125ml/4 fl oz crème fraîche
1 tsp English mustard
salt
freshly ground black pepper

1. Cut the beef into short, thick strips. Heat the oil in a frying pan and fry the meat. The strips should remain pink in the middle. Remove the meat from the pan and keep warm.
2. Peel and chop the onions. Thinly slice the mushrooms.
3. Add the butter to the pan, and melt. Fry the onions until transparent. Add the mushrooms, and fry for 2–3 minutes. Add the wine.
4. Thinly slice the gherkin, and add to the pan. Mix together the crème fraîche and mustard, add to the pan, bring to the boil and allow to reduce a little. Return the meat to the pan, and heat through. Season to taste with salt and pepper.
Serving suggestions: small roast potatoes.
Recommended drinks: a dry white wine.

VIENNESE TAFELSPITZ

SERVES 4-6 ■

Preparation and cooking time: 2–3 hours
Kcal per serving if serving 4: 350
P = 44g, F = 18g, C = 4g

1kg/2¼lbs top rump of beef
500g/1lb 2oz stock bones
2l/3½ pints water
salt
1 leek
1 carrot
½ head celery
1 onion
6 white peppercorns

1. Wash the meat and bones.
2. Bring the water to the boil in a large pan, season lightly with salt and add the soup bones. Trim, wash and slice the leek. Peel and slice the carrot. Trim and slice the celery. Peel the onion.
3. Add the beef, leek, carrot, celery, onion and peppercorns to the pan and bring back to the boil. Cover the pan and lower the heat.
4. Simmer gently for 2–3 hours, skimming off the froth frequently. Transfer the beef to a warm serving dish and cut into finger-thick slices. Strain the cooking liquid and pour a little over the meat before serving.
Serving suggestions: horseradish sauce, roast or boiled potatoes, spinach or leeks.
Recommended drinks: beer or medium red wine.

FRENCH MEATLOAF

SERVES 6 ■

Preparation and cooking time: 1 hour
Kcal per serving: 255
P = 18g, F = 13g, C = 14g

30g/1oz butter
1 onion
150g/5½oz gammon
2 potatoes, peeled and boiled
250g/8oz minced steak
60g/2oz blanched almonds
2 thick slices white bread, crusts removed and soaked in water and squeezed dry
2 eggs, separated
pinch freshly grated nutmeg
1 tsp curry powder
4 tsps brandy
salt

1. Grease a loaf tin.
2. Peel the onion. Coarsely chop the gammon, onion and potatoes in a food processor. Mix the gammon mixture, almonds, bread, egg yolks, nutmeg, curry

Combine the gammon, onion and potatoes in a food processor.

powder, 15g/½oz of the butter and the brandy, and season with salt. Knead thoroughly.
3. Whisk the egg whites and fold into the mixture. Spoon into the loaf tin. Melt the remaining butter and brush over the surface. Bake at 250°C/475°F/Gas Mark 9 for about 30 minutes. Serve hot or cold.
Serving suggestion: salad.
Recommended drink: a hearty red wine.

INDIAN BEEF CURRY

SERVES 4 ■

Preparation and cooking time: 1¼ hours
Marinate overnight
Kcal per serving: 370
P = 26g, F = 29g, C = 1g

500g/1lb 2oz topside of beef
2 tsps salt
2 tsps ground coriander
½ tsp ground turmeric
½ tsp ground cumin
1 tsp chilli powder
½ tsp ground black pepper
1 tbsp chopped fresh root ginger
8 tbsps oil
1 tbsp milk
1 large onion
1–3 garlic cloves
250ml/8 fl oz water
pinch ground cinnamon
pinch ground cloves
1 tbsp chopped fresh coriander leaves

1. Cut the beef into cubes and place in a shallow dish.
2. Combine the salt, ground coriander, turmeric, cumin, chilli powder, pepper, ginger and half the oil. Add the milk and stir to make a smooth paste. Pour over the beef cubes and toss to coat thoroughly. Set aside overnight to marinate.
3. Peel and slice the onion and garlic.
4. Heat the remaining oil, and fry the onion and garlic until golden brown. Add the beef, and fry for 8–10 minutes, stirring frequently, until browned on all sides. Stir in the water.
5. Cover and cook over a low heat for 45 minutes. Add more water if the sauce becomes too thick.
6. Season the curry with the cinnamon and cloves. Transfer to a serving dish and sprinkle with the coriander.
Serving suggestions: fluffy rice and a salad with yogurt dressing.
Recommended drink: a chilled beer.

THAI PORK AND PRAWNS

Nja Tdang

SERVES 4 ■

Preparation and cooking time: 30 minutes
Kcal per serving: 210
P = 25g, F = 11g, C = 3g

3 tbsps dried Chinese
    mushrooms
1 onion
1 garlic clove
2 green chillies
3 tbsps vegetable oil
250g/8oz minced pork
1 tbsp finely chopped root
    ginger
300ml/10 fl oz coconut milk
250g/8oz cooked prawns,
    shelled
1 tbsp soy sauce
2 tbsps fish sauce
½ tsp sugar
salt
1 tbsp chopped coriander
    leaves

1. Rinse the mushrooms, place in a bowl, cover with hot water and set aside to soak for about 10 minutes. Drain well and reserve the soaking liquid.
2. Peel and finely chop the onion and garlic. Seed the chillies. Heat the oil in a wok or frying pan, and stir-fry the minced pork. Add the ginger, garlic and onion, and stir-fry until the onion begins to colour. Stir in the mushrooms and the chillies, and fry for a further 4 minutes.
3. Strain the mushroom soaking liquid through a fine sieve and combine with the coconut milk. Stir the liquid into the pork and onion mixture, and heat through.
4. Add the prawns, and return the liquid to the boil. Add the soy sauce, fish sauce, sugar and, if necessary, season with a little salt. Serve garnished with chopped coriander leaves.
If canned coconut milk is not available, grate some fresh

Virtually all oriental dishes require garlic.

Wash the mushrooms and soak in hot water; they will swell considerably.

Stir-fry all the ingredients in a wok.

coconut or shred in a food processor. Pour over boiling water, allowing 500ml/18 fl oz for each 250g/8oz coconut. Set aside for 15 minutes before straining the liquid through muslin. Desiccated coconut may also be used.
Serving suggestion: rice.

HUNGARIAN GOULASH

SERVES 4 ■ ■

Preparation and cooking time: 1½ hours
Kcal per serving: 600
P = 23g, F = 54g, C = 6g

2 onions
500g/1lb 2oz pork shoulder
    or neck
100g/4oz lard or pork
    dripping
1 tsp sweet paprika
500g/1lb 2oz yellow or green
    peppers
300g/10oz ripe tomatoes
salt

1. Peel and chop the onions. Rinse the pork and pat dry. Dice the pork. Melt the lard or dripping in a flameproof casserole, and stir-fry the onions until transparent. Sprinkle over the paprika and add the pork. Cook over a low heat for 1 hour. If all the liquid evaporates, add 125ml/4 fl oz water.
2. Halve, seed and wash the peppers, and cut into matchstick strips. Blanch, skin and chop the tomatoes. Add the peppers and tomatoes to the casserole. Cover and cook over a low heat for a further 20 minutes. Season to taste with salt and serve.
Serving suggestions: mashed or boiled potatoes.
Recommended drink: a hearty red country wine.

FLORENTINE ROAST PORK

(photograph page 25)

SERVES 6–8 ■

Preparation and cooking time: 2½ hours
Kcal per serving if serving 6: 390
P = 36g, F = 24g, C = 6g

1 x 1.5kgs/3¼lbs boned loin
    of pork
1 garlic clove
1 tbsp fresh rosemary leaves
salt
freshly ground black pepper
4 sprigs fresh rosemary
4 potatoes

1. Rinse the meat and pat dry. Peel the garlic. Chop the rosemary leaves and garlic finely, and season to taste with salt and pepper. Rub the mixture into the pork. Arrange the rosemary sprigs on the joint and tie in place with trussing thread. Attach the pork to a spit with a pan for the juices underneath or place it in a roasting tin.
2. Peel and quarter the potatoes and arrange them in the spit pan or roasting tin. Sprinkle with salt.
3. Spit-roast the pork or roast in a preheated oven at 220°C/450°F/Gas Mark 7 for 2 hours, basting well with the cooking juices. Remove the pork from the spit or the roasting tin, cut the thread and discard the rosemary sprigs. Carve the joint into slices and arrange on a serving dish with the roast potatoes.
Serving suggestion: grilled tomatoes.
Recommended drink: chianti Classico.

MIDDLE EASTERN LEG OF LAMB

SERVES 6 ■
Preparation and cooking time: 2–3 hours
Kcal per serving: 555
P = 35g, F = 36g, C = 23g

1 x 1.5kgs/3¼lbs leg of lamb
3–4 garlic cloves
salt
freshly ground black pepper
3 tbsps olive oil
750g/1lb 11oz potatoes
2 large onions
500g/1lb 2oz tomatoes
1 tsp chopped oregano
1–2 aubergines

Potatoes, tomatoes, onions, aubergines and garlic are cooked with the lamb.

Pierce the flesh with a pointed knife and insert slivers of garlic into the slits.

Add the aubergines when the meat has cooked for 45 minutes.

1. Rinse the lamb and pat dry. Peel and thinly slice the garlic. Pierce the lamb in a number of places with a pointed knife and press slivers of garlic into the slits. Rub plenty of salt and pepper into the flesh. Heat the oil in a large roasting tin and fry the lamb until browned all over. Arrange it in the roasting tin, fatty side down and set aside.
2. Peel and thickly slice the potatoes. Peel the onions and slice the tomatoes. Arrange the potatoes, onions and tomatoes around the meat, and season with salt and pepper. Sprinkle over the oregano.
3. Roast in a preheated oven at 180°C/350°F/Gas Mark 4 for 45 minutes.
4. Meanwhile, wash and slice the aubergines. Sprinkle the slices with salt and set aside for 30 minutes to drain. Pat dry and arrange them around the meat in the roasting tin.
5. Return the roasting tin to the oven for a further 1¼ hours, basting the lamb with the cooking juices from time to time and turning the joint over once. Turn the vegetables once during cooking to ensure that they cook evenly. Spoon out any excess fat. If the vegetables become too dry, a little water may be added.
6. Carve the leg of lamb into slices and arrange on a serving dish with the vegetables.
Serving suggestion: mixed salad.
Recommended drink: a hearty red wine.

TURKISH LAMB MEATBALLS WITH YOGURT

SERVES 4 ■
Preparation and cooking time: 20 minutes
Kcal per serving: 545
P = 31g, F = 42g, C = 10g

3 garlic cloves
600g/1lb 6oz boneless lamb, diced
salt
freshly ground black pepper
2–3 tbsps vegetable oil
2 tsps cornflour
300ml/10 fl oz Greek yogurt
pinch sweet paprika (optional)
8 fresh mint sprigs

1. Peel the garlic, mix with the lamb and chop finely in a food processor. Season to taste with salt and pepper. Shape a number of small meatballs with wet hands, and brush them with oil.
2. Cook the meatballs under a preheated grill until crisp and brown all over. Alternatively, heat the oil in a frying pan, and fry the meatballs until crisp and brown all over. Transfer to a warm serving dish and keep warm.
3. Stir the cornflour into the yogurt in a small saucepan. Gently heat through, stirring constantly. Season with salt.
4. Pour the yogurt over the meatballs and sprinkle with pepper or paprika, if liked, and garnish with the mint.
Serving suggestion: tomato salad.

LAMB NOISETTES WITH TARRAGON

Noisettes d'agneau à l'estragon

SERVES 4 ■
Preparation and cooking time: 20 minutes
Marinate for 12 hours
Kcal per serving: 555
P = 25g, F = 47g, C = 2g

8 x 75g/3oz lamb noisettes
3 tbsps vegetable oil
2 tbsp chopped tarragon
salt
freshly ground black pepper
15g/½oz butter

FOR THE SAUCE:
2 shallots
125ml/4 fl oz white wine
1 tbsp wine vinegar
2 tarragon sprigs
60g/2oz butter, diced

1. Flatten the noisettes to make round steaks. Arrange in a shallow dish. Mix together the oil and tarragon, pour over the lamb and marinate for 12 hours.
2. Drain the noisettes and dry-fry until browned. Turn and season to taste. Add the butter, and fry each side for 3 minutes. Remove from the pan and keep warm.
3. Peel and finely chop the shallots. Add to the wine, vinegar and 1 tarragon sprig. Boil for 5 minutes. Strain.
4. Discard the fat from the roasting tin. Add the wine mixture and place over a low heat, scraping the base of the tin to deglaze. Chop the remaining tarragon, and add to the sauce. Remove from the heat and stir in the butter, 1 piece at a time. Arrange the lamb on a warm serving dish and pour over the sauce.
Serving suggestion: Lyonnaise potatoes.
Recommended drink: a fruity white wine.

DEEP-FRIED MEATBALLS CHINESE STYLE

SERVES 4 ■
Preparation and cooking time: 30 minutes
Kcal per serving: 255
P = 29g, F = 13g, C = 6g

500g/1lb 2oz boneless
    shoulder of pork
½ tsp salt
1 tsp monosodium glutamate
1 tsp rice wine or medium
    sherry
1 tbsp sesame oil
½ tsp finely chopped fresh
    root ginger
2 tsps chopped spring onions
1 egg, lightly beaten
2 tbsps cornflour
1 tbsp water
oil for deep-frying

1. Finely chop the pork. Mix together the pork, salt, monosodium glutamate, rice wine or sherry, sesame oil, ginger, onions, egg, 2 tsps of the cornflour and the water. Knead thoroughly to make a smooth mixture.
2. Shape the mixture into small meatballs, and dip them in the remaining cornflour.
3. Heat the oil in a wok or frying pan, and stir-fry the meatballs for about 5 minutes until they are golden brown all over. Drain and serve immediately.
The pork for these meatballs should not be ground finely in a meat mincer but minced in a food processor. In this way the meat fibres are not so badly damaged.
Serving suggestions: rice and Chinese cabbage.
Recommended drinks: beer, a dry rosé wine or China tea.

CANTONESE FONDUE

(photograph page 40)

SERVES 10 ■ ■
Preparation and cooking time: 2 hours
Kcal per serving: 315
P = 31g, F = 17g, C = 12g

250g/8oz beef sirloin
250g/8oz lamb fillet
250g/8oz pork fillet
150g/5½oz pig's liver or pig's
    kidneys
200g/7oz fish fillet
10 cubes tofu
1 small Chinese cabbage
10 thin spring onions
100g/4oz cellophane noodles,
    soaked
200g/7oz raw prawns, shelled

FOR THE DIP:
12 tbsps soy sauce
1 tsp ground ginger
2 tbsps finely chopped
    shallots
6 tbsps soya oil
2 tbsps finely chopped fresh
    parsley

FOR THE STOCK:
1.5l/2½ pints chicken stock
4 slices fresh root ginger
salt
freshly ground white pepper

1. Place the beef, lamb and pork in the freezer until partially frozen. Cut into wafer-thin slices. Spread them out on a large dish. Blanch the liver or kidneys in boiling water for 2 minutes and then plunge straight into cold water. Thinly slice. Thinly slice the fish fillet. Soak the tofu in cold water for 1 minute, drain and cut in quarters. Wash and shred the cabbage. Trim and wash the spring onions. Strain the noodles. Arrange all the ingredients attractively on dishes.
2. To make the dip, mix together all the ingredients in a small pan and bring to the boil. Divide the dip between 10 small bowls.

Cut the meat into wafer-thin slices. Cut the fish into thicker slices.

Cellophane noodles, spring onions, tofu, ginger and Chinese cabbage are classic ingredients in Chinese cooking.

3. To prepare the stock, place the chicken stock and root ginger in an earthenware fondue pan. Season to taste with salt and pepper, and bring to the boil. Transfer the fondue pan to the burner.
4. Arrange all the prepared ingredients around the fondue and place a soup bowl and a dish of the dip in front of each guest.
5. Each guest chooses their ingredients, holding them with a fondue fork or chopsticks. They are then dipped first into the boiling stock until cooked, and then the dip. Finally the stock is drunk as a soup from the bowls.
Serving suggestion: prawn crackers.
Recommended drinks: China tea or rice wine.

MIXED GRILL

SERVES 4 ■
Preparation and cooking time: 30 minutes
Marinate for 2 hours
Kcal per serving: 605
P = 33g, F = 52g, C = 0g

4 small slices beef fillet
4 lamb cutlets
1–2 tbsps oil
4 small veal fillet slices
4 small pork sausages or 4
    small slices calf's liver
4 thin rashers streaky bacon
salt
freshly ground black pepper

FOR THE MARINADE:
1 garlic clove
5 tbsps oil
½ tsp black peppercorns,
    crushed

1. First make the marinade. Peel and crush the garlic. Mix together the oil, garlic and crushed peppercorns. Brush the marinade over the beef fillet slices and the lamb cutlets, and set aside in the refrigerator for 2 hours. Turn the meat over occasionally.
2. Brush the grill pan with a little oil and pre-heat.
3. Brush some of the marinade over the veal and liver, if using. Arrange the meat, sausages or liver and bacon side-by-side on the grill pan, and grill on both sides until golden brown. After turning, season with salt and pepper. Brush with some of the marinade from time to time. The meat should be tender when pressed, and all but the sausages should still be pink in the middle.
4. Arrange the cooked meat slices on a wooden platter or a large serving dish.
Serving suggestions: foil-wrapped baked potatoes, grilled tomatoes and herb butter.
Recommended drink: a hearty red wine.

Cooking for Special Occasions

When lovers of fine food are in the mood for meat, then classical haute cuisine recipes will be on the menu. Inevitably tender pieces of beef, veal and lamb will be most in demand, and yet it could just as easily be a pork spare-rib joint that has absorbed the delicate flavours of a spicy white wine marinade. Many people prefer not to feast on large roasts or huge steaks – there are, after all, other things to enjoy apart from meat – but the meat course is often the highlight of a special occasion meal. Moreover, the cook will invariably be judged by his or her ability to create something special from top-quality ingredients. This chapter offers a selection of the best classical meat recipes.

Sirloin Steaks with Anchovy Cream (recipe page 58)

MUSTARD BEEF

SERVES 6 ■ ■ ■

Preparation and cooking time: 1½ hours
Marinate for 2 days
Kcal per serving: 500
P = 31g, F = 34g, C = 1g

1 x 1.25kgs/2¾lbs forerib of
  beef
1 garlic clove
1 small hot chilli pepper
500ml/18 fl oz red wine
1 bay leaf
1 tbsp rosemary leaves
salt
freshly ground black pepper
2 tbsps olive oil
2 tbsps Dijon mustard

Boil the red wine and spices and then leave to cool.

1. Rinse the meat and pat dry. Place in a dish.
2. Peel and crush the garlic. Seed and wash the chilli. Place the wine, garlic, chilli, bay leaf and rosemary in a small pan, and season with pepper. Bring to the boil, remove from the heat and set aside to cool.
3. When the mixture is cool, pour it over the meat and set aside in the refrigerator for 36 hours, turning the joint two or three times each day.

Cover the meat with the cold marinade and leave to stand in the refrigerator for 1½ days.

475°F/Gas Mark 9. Sprinkle with salt and coat with the mustard.
5. Return the beef to the oven and roast for 40 minutes, basting frequently, until it is pink. Just before it is ready, cover with aluminium foil.
6. Before carving, turn off the oven and leave the beef to stand for 3–4 minutes, so that all the juice does not run out when it is cut.
7. Dilute the meat juices with the marinade, bring to the boil and allow to reduce. Serve the gravy separately.
Serving suggestions: gratin dauphinois and a mixed salad.
Recommended drink: a good Burgundy wine.

> ### TIP
> *Forerib generally refers to ribs 6 to 12 and this cut should ideally be served rare to medium.*
> *Use a meat thermometer to check whether the meat is cooked according to your requirements.*

4. Remove the beef from the marinade, pat dry and brush with oil. Reserve the marinade. Place the beef in a roasting tin and brown in a preheated oven at 250°C/

ENTRECÔTE WITH CHERVIL SAUCE

SERVES 2 ■ ■

Preparation and cooking time: 30–35 minutes
Kcal per serving: 420
P = 24g, F = 35g, C = 2g

1 x 300g/10oz entrecôte steak
salt
freshly ground black pepper
1 shallot
40g/1½oz butter
2 tsps chopped fresh chervil
2 small courgettes
½ tsp paprika
5 tbsps double cream
pinch cayenne pepper

Make a number of cuts in the fatty edge of the steak so that it retains its shape when fried.

1. Remove the steak from the refrigerator 30 minutes before it is required. Pat dry and score the rind a number of times so that it does not contract when cooked. Rub salt into the flesh, sprinkle generously with pepper, cover and leave to stand at room temperature.
2. Meanwhile, peel and chop the shallot. Melt 15g/½ oz of the butter in a frying pan, and gently fry the shallot and half the chervil. Remove from the heat and set aside.
3. Melt the remaining butter in another pan, and fry the steak for 6–7 minutes on each side. Make sure that it remains pink in the middle. For a rare steak, 3–4 minutes on each side is sufficient. Once the steak has been turned over, sprinkle with salt. Wrap the steak in aluminium foil when cooked.
4. Wash, peel and chop the courgettes. Place them in the meat juices over a high heat. Sprinkle over the paprika and stir-fry until very little of the liquid remains.
5. Add the shallot mixture and the cream to the pan and boil, stirring constantly, until it reaches a thick and creamy consistency. Season

Wrap the entrecôte in aluminium foil while preparing the sauce.

with salt and cayenne pepper.
6. Cut the steak across the fibres into 1cm/½-inch slices. Pour the sauce onto warmed plates and arrange the meat slices on top. Sprinkle over the remaining chervil.
Serving suggestions: sliced roast potatoes and mixed vegetables.
Recommended drink: a medium red wine.

> ### TIP
> *Cook the courgettes at the highest heat possible to prevent the liquid from escaping.*

BEEF FILLETS WITH CEPS AND RED WINE SAUCE

SERVES 4 ■ ■
*Preparation and cooking
time: 40 minutes
Kcal per serving: 355
P = 36g, F = 18g, C = 2g*

3 shallots or 1 onion
60g/2oz butter
20g/⅚oz dried ceps
250ml/8 fl oz red wine
3 tbsps concentrated beef
    stock
4 x 150g/5½oz beef fillets
salt
freshly ground black pepper
1 tsp chopped fresh parsley

1. Peel and finely chop the shallots or onion. Melt 15g/½oz of the butter, and stir-fry the shallots for 5 minutes. Remove from the heat and set aside.
2. Place the ceps in a bowl, cover with water and set aside to soak.
3. Place half the shallots and 200ml/6 fl oz of the wine in a small pan. Bring to the boil and allow to reduce by half.

> ### TIP
> *If using fresh ceps, do not add them to the sauce, but fry them quickly in butter just before serving.*

4. Drain the ceps and add to the reduced wine. Add the remaining wine and the stock, bring to the boil and allow to reduce by half.
5. Melt 15g/½oz of the remaining butter, and fry the beef until rare or medium, according to taste. Season with salt and pepper and arrange on a warm serving dish. Add the reserved shallots.

Combine half the cooked shallots with 200ml/6 fl oz red wine and allow to reduce by half.

Add the soaked ceps to the concentrated beef stock and reduce by half again.

Beat the diced butter into the red wine sauce.

6. Dice the remaining butter. Remove the sauce from the heat and allow to cool slightly. Beat in the butter a few pieces at a time. Continue to beat until the sauce is light and creamy. Season the beef fillets again with salt and pepper, if necessary, pour over the sauce and sprinkle with parsley.
Serving suggestions: cream potatoes and fresh green vegetables.
Recommended drink: a good full-bodied red wine.

FILLET OF BEEF IN SHERRY VINEGAR

SERVES 4 ■ ■
*Preparation and cooking
time: 50 minutes
Kcal per serving: 265
P = 29g, F = 16g, C = 3g*

40g/1½oz butter
1 x 600g/1lb 6oz fillet of beef
2 tbsps sherry vinegar
2 kiwi fruits
125ml/4 fl oz veal stock or a
    thin stock
1 garlic clove
1 tbsp tomato purée
pinch sugar
pinch cayenne pepper
salt
freshly ground black pepper

1. Melt 15g/½oz of the butter, and fry the beef until browned on all sides. Add the sherry vinegar and scrape the base of the pan with a spatula to deglaze. Partially cover and cook for a further 10 minutes. Remove the fillet from the frying pan and keep warm.
2. Peel the kiwi fruits. Dice 1 and slice the other. Purée the diced kiwi fruit and the stock in a blender.
3. Peel and crush the garlic clove. Add the garlic to the sherry vinegar mixture, and stir in the kiwi fruit mixture, tomato purée, sugar and cayenne pepper over a low heat. Season with salt and pepper and remove the pan from the heat.
4. Dice the remaining butter and stir into the sauce. Pour onto warmed plates.
5. Cut the fillet into slices and arrange on the sauce. Garnish with kiwi fruit slices.
Serving suggestions: rice and leaf spinach.
Recommended drink: a red or white country wine.

SIRLOIN STEAKS WITH ANCHOVY CREAM

(photograph page 54)

SERVES 4 ■ ■
*Preparation and cooking
time: 15–20 minutes
Kcal per serving: 390
P = 31g, F = 26g, C = 1g*

15g/½oz butter
4 x 150g/5½oz sirloin steaks

FOR THE SAUCE:
125ml/4 fl oz ruby port
3 anchovy fillets
4 tbsps double cream
1 garlic clove
60g/2oz butter
salt
freshly ground black pepper
1 tbsp chopped fresh basil

FOR THE GARNISH:
4 anchovy fillets
4 black olives

1. Melt the butter, and fry the steaks for 2–3 minutes on each side until rare or medium, according to taste. Remove from the pan and keep warm.
2. Add the port to the pan, bring to the boil and allow to reduce by half.
3. Drain the anchovy fillets and pat dry. Chop finely and mash or purée in a blender.
4. Crush the garlic clove and combine with the anchovy purée, cream and reduced port. Allow to reduce again until the sauce is light and creamy.
5. Lower the heat. Dice the butter, and stir into the sauce. Season to taste with salt and pepper, and stir in the basil. Remember that anchovies are very salty.
6. Arrange the steaks on warmed plates, pour over the sauce and garnish each with an anchovy and an olive.
Serving suggestion: courgettes.
Recommended drink: chianti Classico.

ROLLED BREAST OF VEAL

SERVES 3 ■ ■

Preparation and cooking time: 45–50 minutes
Kcal per serving: 385
P = 39g, F = 22g, C = 1g

100g/4oz mushrooms
1 x 600g/1lb 6oz boned breast
    of veal
2 garlic cloves
40g/1½oz butter
2 tbsps finely chopped fresh
    mixed herbs
salt
freshly ground black pepper
250ml/8 fl oz white wine
125ml/4 fl oz stock

1. Chop the mushrooms. Rinse the breast of veal, pat dry and lay out on the work top.
2. Crush the garlic. Melt 15g/½oz of the butter, and gently fry the garlic, herbs and mushrooms.
3. Spread the mixture over the veal, and season to taste with salt and pepper. Roll up the veal and secure with trussing thread.
4. Melt the remaining butter in a flameproof casserole, and fry the veal until browned all over. Season again with salt and pepper.
5. Roast the veal in a pre-heated oven at 180–200°C/350–400°F/Gas Mark 4–6 for 25–30 minutes. From time to time add a little wine.
6. Remove the veal from the casserole, place on a large serving dish and remove the trussing thread. Keep warm. Add the stock to the cooking juices, set over a medium heat and allow to reduce.
7. Remove the thread and carve the rolled veal at the table. Pour over a little gravy.
Serving suggestions: potato pancakes and fresh green vegetables.
Recommended drink: a red country wine.

Gently fry the mushrooms, crushed garlic and chopped herbs in butter.

Spread the mixture on the breast of veal.

Roll up the veal starting at the narrow end. Ensure that the filling does not squeeze out at the sides.

Secure the veal roll with trussing thread.

VEAL ESCALOPES WITH SWEET AND SOUR SAUCE

SERVES 4 ■ ■

Preparation and cooking time: 45 minutes
Kcal per serving: 170
P = 21g, F = 4g, C = 7g

1 carrot
1 onion
300g/10oz veal bones,
    crushed
½ bay leaf
1 clove
4 x 100g/4oz thin veal
    escalopes
15g/½oz butter
salt
freshly ground black pepper
1 tbsp sugar
3 tbsps lemon juice
1 garlic clove
1 tsp grated lemon peel
1 tbsp tomato purée
1 tsp cornflour
2 tsps soy sauce
2 tbsps white wine or sherry
pinch cayenne pepper

1. Peel and dice the carrot. Peel and coarsely chop the onion. Place the bones in a pan with 250ml/8 fl oz water, the carrot, onion, bay leaf and clove, bring to the boil and simmer for 20 minutes. Strain and return to the pan. Bring to the boil and reduce to 6 tbsps.
2. Melt the butter, and fry the veal until browned on both sides. Remove from the pan, season with salt and pepper and keep warm.
3. Place the sugar in a small pan and heat gently until it becomes runny. Stir well and allow to caramelise. Add 1 tbsp stock, followed by 1 tbsp lemon juice.
4. Add the meat juices to the remaining stock and heat through. Peel and crush the garlic. Add to the stock together with the caramel, lemon peel, tomato purée and remaining lemon juice. Season with salt and pepper, and bring to the boil.

The veal escalopes should be very thin. If necessary, flatten with a steak hammer.

5. Stir together the cornflour, soy sauce and white wine or sherry and add to the sweet and sour sauce. Continue to boil until the sauce starts to thicken. Season with cayenne pepper, and pour the sauce over the meat.
Serving suggestions: rice, broccoli or mangetout.
Recommended drink: rosé wine.

TIP

The veal escalopes should be very thin. If necessary, place them in a polythene bag and flatten them with a steak hammer.
As an alternative, replace the veal with thinly sliced turkey escalopes.

VEAL IN A ROASTING BAG

SERVES 4 ■■
Preparation and cooking time: 50 minutes
Kcal per serving: 280
P = 33g, F = 15g, C = 3g

1 x 600g/1lb 6oz shoulder of
   veal
salt
freshly ground black pepper
60g/2oz streaky bacon, cut in
   thin rashers, rinded
10 sage leaves
2 carrots
1 stick celery
pinch ground mace
1 small garlic clove, peeled
1 onion, studded with 1 clove
1 bay leaf
4 tbsps veal stock
1 tbsp tomato purée
20g/¾oz butter

Make deep cuts in the top of the joint and place a little bacon and sage between the slices.

Tie the veal joint together with trussing thread.

1. Rinse the veal and pat dry. Make deep cuts in the veal at 1.5–2cm/½–¾-inch intervals. Sprinkle pepper between the slices and then tuck a small piece of bacon and a small sage leaf (or half a leaf) in the cuts. Tie the joint together lengthways with trussing thread.
2. Peel and chop the carrots. Trim and chop the celery.
3. Cut a length of roasting bag 1½ times the length of the joint and seal one end.
4. Rub the mace and salt into the flesh, place the joint into the bag and add the garlic, onion, bay leaf, carrot and celery. Seal the bag and pierce a number of holes with a pointed knife.
5. Place the roasting bag on a baking tray, and cook the veal in a preheated oven at 220°C/425°F/Gas Mark 7 for 35 minutes.
6. Remove the bag from the oven and cut open the top. Pour the meat juices into a small pan. Turn off the oven and place the meat inside to keep warm.
7. Add the stock to the meat juices, bring to the boil and

Place the meat and vegetables inside the roasting bag and seal the ends tightly.

allow to reduce by a half. Add the tomato purée, season with salt and pepper and remove from the heat. Dice the butter and stir into the gravy one piece at a time. Carve the veal and arrange on a warm serving plate and hand the gravy separately.
Serving suggestions: risotto or noodles.
Recommended drink: chianti Classico.

KNUCKLE OF VEAL IN ORANGE SAUCE

(photograph page 15)

SERVES 4 ■■
Preparation and cooking time: 1 hour 50 minutes
Marinate overnight
Kcal per serving: 385
P = 54g, F = 12g, C = 11g

1 orange
2 garlic cloves
1 carrot
100g/4oz onions
3 tbsps olive oil
2 tbsps lemon juice
125ml/4 fl oz orange juice
3–4 allspice berries
4 slices knuckle of veal
   (about 1kg/2¼lbs)
salt
freshly ground black pepper
1 bay leaf
120ml/4 fl oz white wine
½ tsp meat extract
pinch cayenne pepper
1 tbsp chopped fresh parsley

1. Wash the orange, peel thinly and chop the peel finely. Peel and crush the garlic. Peel and chop the carrot and onions.
2. Mix together 2 tbsps of the olive oil, the lemon juice, orange juice, garlic, carrot, onion, orange peel and allspice berries.
3. Rinse the veal slices and pat dry. Sprinkle generously with pepper and then dip them in the orange marinade. Place them in a shallow dish and pour over the remaining marinade. Add the bay leaf and set aside in the refrigerator overnight.
4. Remove the veal from the marinade, scraping off the bits with a spatula. Reserve the marinade. Heat the remaining olive oil in a flameproof casserole, and fry the veal until browned on all sides. Season with salt and pepper.
5. Add the reserved marinade, cover and cook gently

Wash the orange well, peel it thinly and chop the peel finely.

Sprinkle the veal slices with pepper, cover with the marinade and refrigerate overnight.

Remove the veal from the marinade, scraping off the bits with a spatula.

for 1½ hours, gradually adding the wine during the cooking time. Transfer the veal to a warm serving dish.
6. Stir the meat extract into the sauce, and season with salt and cayenne pepper. Remove and discard the bay leaf. Pour the sauce over the veal and serve garnished with the chopped parsley.
Serving suggestions: fried courgettes and rice.
Recommended drink: a light

PORK SPARE RIB IN WHITE WINE

SERVES 4 ■
Preparation and cooking time: 3 hours 25 minutes
Marinate for 1–2
Kcal per serving: 645
P = 35g, F = 37g, C = 10g

800g/1¾lbs lean pork spare rib
2 large onions
1 clove
1 carrot
1 small leek
60g/2oz celery
1 bay leaf
1 thyme sprig
1 rosemary sprig
1 sage sprig
1 marjoram sprig
1 basil sprig
1 bottle white wine
30g/1oz butter
salt
freshly ground black pepper
6 tbsps double cream
150g/5½oz mushrooms

1. Place the pork in a deep dish. Peel 1 onion, stud with the clove and add to the dish. Peel and chop the carrot. Trim, wash and chop the leek and celery. Peel and chop the remaining onion.
2. Add the carrot, leek, celery, chopped onion, bay leaf, thyme, rosemary, sage, marjoram and basil to the dish. Pour over sufficient wine just to cover the pork. Set aside for 1–2 days to marinate, turning the joint each day.
3. Remove the pork from the marinade. Rub the marinade through a sieve into a pan, bring to the boil and skim off any froth. Reserve the vegetables.
4. Pat the pork dry. Heat half the butter in a roasting tin and brown the pork all over. Remove from the tin and stir the reserved vegetables into the pan juices.
5. Season the pork with salt and pepper and then return it to the roasting tin. Add half

the marinade and cook in a preheated oven at its lowest setting (80°C/175°F/Low) for 3 hours. Add a little more marinade from time to time.
6. Transfer the pork to a large dish and cover with foil. Switch off the oven and leave the meat to rest for 10 minutes.
7. Meanwhile, strain the sauce into a frying pan, bring to the boil and allow to reduce slightly. Stir in the cream, bring to the boil again and season with salt and pepper, if necessary.
8. Wipe and slice the mushrooms. Melt the remaining butter, and gently fry the mushrooms.
9. Cut the meat into 1cm/½-inch slices and arrange on a serving dish. Top with the mushrooms. Serve the sauce separately.
Serving suggestion: mashed potato or green noodles.
Recommended drink: a vin de pays.

> **TIP**
>
> *The special flavour of this pork derives from the wine marinade and the herbs and vegetables. For this reason a lengthy period of marinating is essential, even as long as 5 days.*

PORK STEAKS WITH AVOCADO SAUCE

SERVES 4 ■ ■
Preparation and cooking time: 40 minutes
Kcal per serving: 725
P = 31g, F = 66g, C = 2g

2 ripe avocados
2 tbsps lemon juice
4 x 150g/5½oz pork steaks
salt
freshly ground black pepper
60g/2oz butter
250ml/9 fl oz chicken stock
4 tbsps double cream
2 tsps curry powder
pinch cayenne pepper

1. Peel and stone the avocado pears. Brush the flesh of 1 avocado with lemon juice. Purée the other with a hand-held mixer or mash with a fork.

The avocado can be puréed with a hand-held blender.

2. Sprinkle the steaks with pepper. Melt the butter, and fry the pork until golden. Remove from the pan. Stir the stock into the meat juices and bring to the boil.
3. Combine the avocado purée and cream. Add the mixture to the stock, and season with curry powder, salt and cayenne. Warm through but do not boil.
4. Warm the steaks in the sauce for 1–2 minutes. Slice the peeled avocado and arrange on the steaks.
Serving suggestion: rice.
Recommended drink: a red country wine.

PORK CHOPS WITH SOUR CREAM SAUCE

SERVES 4 ■ ■
Preparation and cooking time: 35–40 minutes
Kcal per serving: 640
P = 34g, F = 52g, C = 8g

30g/1oz butter
1 tbsp capers
4 x 200g/7oz pork chops
salt
freshly ground white pepper
4 tbsps chopped onions
2 tbsps white wine vinegar
1 tbsp clear honey
250ml/9 fl oz sour cream
1 tbsp chopped gherkins
2 tsps chopped fresh tarragon
2 tsps English mustard
1 tsp wholegrain mustard

1. Rinse the capers in cold water.
2. Melt the butter, and fry the chops until golden brown on both sides. Season with salt and pepper, partially cover and cook for 10–12 minutes. Remove from the pan and keep warm.
3. Pour off any excess fat. Add the onions to the pan, and gently fry for 2–3 minutes. Stir in the vinegar and honey.
4. Stir in the cream, bring to the boil and season with salt and pepper. Add the gherkins, half the tarragon, the English mustard and the wholegrain mustard. Mix thoroughly. Do not allow to boil.
5. Arrange the chops on a warm serving dish and pour over the sauce. Garnish with the remaining tarragon and the rinsed capers.
Serving suggestion: noodles, mashed potato or rice.
Recommended drink: beer or a red country wine.

HERBED RACK OF LAMB

SERVES 4 ■ ■
*Preparation and cooking
time: 50 minutes
Kcal per serving: 995
P = 37g, F = 88g, C = 6g*

1 x 1.25kgs/2¾lbs rib of lamb
  with bones
60g/2oz butter
salt
freshly ground black pepper
2 garlic bulbs
1 carrot
1 tomato
250ml/9 fl oz Marsala
5 tbsps chopped fresh parsley
2 tbsps chopped mixed fresh
  herbs
2 tbsps butter

*Roast the halved garlic bulbs,
carrot and tomato with the lamb.*

*Scoop the garlic cloves out of the
bulb with a teaspoon.*

1. Rinse the lamb and pat dry. Melt half the butter in a flameproof casserole, and brown the lamb in a preheated oven at 200°C/400°F/Gas Mark 6, turning from time to time. Season with salt and pepper. Cut the garlic bulbs in half and place, face down, on the base of the casserole. Peel the carrot. Add the carrot and tomato to the casserole, cover and cook for a further 5 minutes.

> **TIP**
>
> *Ask your butcher
> to chine the lamb
> to make carving
> a little easier.
> For really special
> occasions, use a
> whole loin of
> lamb (2.5kgs/
> 5½lbs is sufficient
> for 8 people).*

2. Partially uncover the casserole and cook the meat for a further 10 minutes, gradually adding the Marsala during the cooking time.
3. Switch off the oven and leave the lamb to rest for 5 minutes.
4. Meanwhile, remove the garlic bulbs and scoop out the flesh with a teaspoon. Mix the garlic, parsley and mixed herbs. Melt the remaining butter in a frying pan, and gently fry the garlic and herb mixture for 5–6 minutes.
5. Transfer the lamb to a warm serving dish and coat the outer surface with a smooth layer of the herb mixture. Carve the joint at the table.
Serving suggestions: Lyonnaise potatoes and broccoli.
Recommended drink: rosé or a medium red wine.

LEG OF LAMB WITH ROSEMARY

(photograph page 19)

SERVES 3–4 ■ ■
*Preparation and cooking
time: 1¼ hours
Kcal per serving if serving 4:
790
P = 46g, F = 61g, C = 5g*

1 x 1.25kgs/2¾lbs leg of lamb
2–3 tbsps rosemary leaves
salt
freshly ground black pepper
75g/3oz butter
2 carrots
2 tomatoes
1 celery sprig
2 garlic cloves
1 bay leaf
250ml/8 fl oz white wine

*Pierce holes in the lamb and stud
with rosemary leaves.*

*Carve the meat into 1cm/½-inch
slices.*

1. Ask your butcher to remove the layer of fat from the leg of lamb. It may also be necessary to ask him to shorten the bones so that it fits into the roasting tin, but ask to keep the bones.
2. Wash the lamb and pat dry. Pierce a series of holes about 2–3cm/¾–1 inch deep with a larding needle. Insert a rosemary leaf into each hole. Season with salt and pepper.
3. Melt 30g/1oz of the butter in a roasting tin, add the lamb and any bones, baste with the melted butter and roast in a preheated oven at 180°C/350°F/Gas Mark 4.
4. Peel the carrots and cut in half lengthways. Halve the tomatoes. Add the carrots, tomatoes, celery sprig, unpeeled garlic cloves and bay leaf to the roasting tin.
5. Cover the meat with foil and roast for 45–50 minutes, gradually adding the wine during the cooking.
6. Switch off the oven. Transfer the lamb to a warm plate and return to the oven to rest for a further 8 minutes.
7. Strain the meat juices into a small pan. Add 3–4 tbsps water to the roasting tin, bring to the boil and pour into the pan. Set over a low heat. Dice the remaining butter and beat into the cooking juices. Warm through, beating constantly, but do not boil. Season well and pour into a warmed gravy boat.
8. Serve the carrots with the lamb, if liked, but discard the bay leaf and garlic cloves.
9. Carve the meat at the table. First remove the upper and lower 'eye' from the bone. Place the joint across the carving board and cut diagonal slices. The flesh should still be pink.
Serving suggestion: roast potatoes.
Recommended drink: a full-bodied red wine.

Wholefood Recipes

*M*eat normally occupies only a small place in wholefood recipe books, but these splendid recipes by Doris Katharina Hessler for beef, veal, lamb and other meats go some way towards redressing the balance. Naturally, all the ingredients are fresh and require very short cooking times. Delicious vegetables, mushrooms, sweetcorn and rice are combined to create healthy and tasty dishes. Of course, cereal grains, sprouts, pulses and nuts accompany the meat, not to mention a range of aromatics, herbs and spices – each used sparingly but with an important part to play in enhancing the meat's flavour. Inevitably the outcome will be not only wholesome and natural, but imaginative and unusual.

Loin of Lamb with Pistou au Gratin (recipe page 78)

69

BEEF FILLET IN GORGONZOLA SAUCE

SERVES 4 ■
Preparation and cooking time: 30 minutes
Kcal per serving: 595
P = 34g, F = 48g, C = 2g

400ml/14 fl oz home-made beef stock
200ml/7 fl oz double cream
60g/2oz butter
3 tbsps medium sherry
4 tsps sherry vinegar
1 x 500g/1lb 2oz fillet of beef
salt
freshly ground white pepper
3 tbsps grapeseed oil
150g–200g/5–7oz Gorgonzola cheese
2 tbsps whipping cream, whipped

Brown the beef on all sides.

1. Place the stock, double cream, butter, sherry and vinegar in a pan. Bring to the boil over a medium heat and allow to reduce by a third.
2. Season the beef with salt and pepper. Heat the oil in a flameproof casserole, and brown the beef all over. Transfer the casserole to a preheated oven and cook at 200°C/400°F/Gas Mark 6 for 10 minutes. Remove the beef, wrap in foil and leave to rest for 10 minutes.

When cooked, wrap the fillet in foil for 10 minutes.

3. Dice the Gorgonzola cheese, and add to the reduced sauce. Purée with a hand blender and then rub through a sieve. Return to the pan, bring to the boil and add the whipped cream.
4. Cut the beef into slices and arrange on a serving plate. Hand the sauce separately.
Serving suggestions: whole-wheat noodles, broccoli or leaf spinach.
Recommended drink: a hearty white wine.

Purée the sauce and diced Gorgonzola with a hand blender and rub it through a sieve.

Cut the fillet into slices with a carving knife. Hand the sauce separately.

BEEF FILLETS ON A BED OF CREAMY VEGETABLES IN RED WINE AND MADEIRA SAUCE

SERVES 4 ■ ■ ■
Preparation and cooking time: 50 minutes
Kcal per serving: 785
P = 22g, F = 57g, C = 18g

4 x 80g/3oz beef fillets
salt
freshly ground white pepper
2 tbsps oil

FOR THE CREAMY VEGETABLES:
100g/4oz carrots
100g/4oz kohlrabi
100g/4oz celery
100g/4oz leeks
20g/⅔oz butter or margarine
salt
freshly ground white pepper
150ml/5 fl oz double cream
125ml/4 fl oz chicken stock
3 tbsps white port
100g/4oz mushrooms, preferably Japanese enoki mushrooms
1 60g/2oz black truffle

FOR THE SAUCE:
2 shallots
250ml/8 fl oz red wine
250ml/8 fl oz Madeira
4 tsps balsamic or red wine vinegar

TO SERVE:
150g/5½oz butter
2 tbsps whipping cream, whipped

1. First make the creamy vegetables. Peel the carrots and kohlrabi. Trim and wash the celery and leeks. Cut all the vegetables into match-stick strips.
2. Melt the butter or margarine in a flameproof casserole, and gently fry the vegetables. Season with salt and pepper, and then stir in the cream, stock and port. Wipe the mushrooms. Cut the truffle into thin strips.

Cut all the vegetables into matchstick strips and fry gently in the butter or margarine.

Add the mushrooms and truffle to the cream mixture, and allow to reduce slightly.
3. To make the red wine sauce, peel and chop the shallots. Mix together the wine, Madeira and vinegar in a small pan. Bring to the boil and allow to reduce to a quarter.
4. Meanwhile, pat the beef dry, and season. Heat the oil, and brown both sides of the beef. Lower the heat, and fry for a further 5 minutes. Remove the pan from the heat and set aside.
5. Rub the reduced red wine sauce through a sieve. Dice 100g/4oz of the butter, and beat into the sauce, a few pieces at a time. Mix the remaining butter with the vegetables. Finally fold the whipped cream into the vegetables.
6. Serve the vegetables on a warm dish and top with the fillets. Pour over the sauce.
Recommended drink: a fruity red wine.

> **TIP**
>
> *Enoki mushrooms, are a Japanese delicacy. They are very tiny. If you cannot find them, use the smallest button mushrooms.*

BEEF FILLET AND CHANTERELLES WRAPPED IN SWISS CHARD LEAVES

SERVES 4 ■■
Preparation and cooking time: 1 hour
Kcal per serving: 345
P = 21g, F = 26g, C = 8g

400g/14oz chanterelle
 mushrooms
2 shallots
40g/1½oz butter
salt
freshly ground white pepper
100ml/3 fl oz double cream
3 tbsps finely chopped fresh
 parsley
1–2 tbsps breadcrumbs
4 x 80g/3oz beef fillets
2 tbsps oil
4 large Swiss chard leaves

Add sufficient breadcrumbs to the mushroom filling to bind the mixture together.

Wrap the beef fillet first in a Swiss chard leaf and then a sheet of aluminium foil.

1. Wipe the chanterelles and cut into small pieces. Peel and chop the shallots. Melt the butter in a flameproof casserole, and gently fry the chanterelles and shallots for 5 minutes. Season with salt and pepper and stir in the cream. Bring to the boil and allow to reduce slightly. Stir in the parsley, and add sufficient breadcrumbs to bind the mixture, which should be of a workable consistency. Remove from the heat and set aside to cool.

> ### TIP
> *If chanterelles are not available, almost any wild or cultivated mushroom, such as shiitake or cloud ears, would be suitable for the filling.*

2. Pat the fillets dry, and season with salt and pepper. Heat the oil in a frying pan, and fry the fillet slices over a high heat for 2 minutes on each side. Remove and set aside to cool.
3. Bring a large pan of lightly salted water to the boil. Blanch the Swiss chard leaves, remove and plunge them straight into ice-cold water. Lay the leaves out on a tea-towel and dry them well. Coat each leaf with some of the mushroom filling and place a fillet slice on top. Wrap the fillet tightly first in the Swiss chard leaf and then in a sheet of aluminium foil. Poach for 8–10 minutes in lightly boiling water.
Serving suggestions: chive sauce and small white turnips.
Recommended drink: a hearty white wine.

BEEF FILLETS IN MORELLO CHERRY SAUCE

SERVES 4 ■■
Preparation and cooking time: 40 minutes
Kcal per serving: 450
P = 20g, F = 28g, C = 21g

200g/7oz baby onions
salt
freshly ground white pepper
400g/14oz morello cherries
2 shallots
250ml/8 fl oz beef stock
125ml/4 fl oz red wine
125ml/4 fl oz kirsch or cherry
 brandy
60ml/2 fl oz port
4 x 75g/3oz slices beef fillet
4 tbsps grapeseed oil
1 tsp arrowroot
40g/1½oz butter

1. Peel the baby onions. Blanch in lightly salted boiling water for 1 minute. Drain. Wash and stone the cherries.
2. Peel and chop the shallots. Place the shallots, stock, wine, kirsch or cherry brandy and port in a small pan and bring to the boil over a high heat. Allow to reduce by a third.

> ### TIP
> *For best results use fresh cherries for this dish, but in winter frozen or canned and drained morello cherries are a suitable alternative. This sauce also goes well with game.*

3. Meanwhile, pat the beef dry, and season with salt and pepper. Heat half the oil in a frying pan, and fry the beef for about 2 minutes on each side. Remove from the pan,

Fry the fillets in the oil, turning to brown both sides.

Add the remaining cherries to the sauce just before serving.

wrap in aluminium foil and set aside to rest.
4. Add the remaining oil to the pan, and fry the baby onions over a high heat. Season with salt and pepper. Add 300g/10oz of the cherries and warm through.
5. Rub the reduced sauce through a sieve into a pan. Bring back to the boil and stir in the arrowroot. Dice the butter, and stir into the sauce, a few pieces at a time. Add the remaining cherries.
6. Place the steaks on warm plates and surround with the onions and cherries. Pour over the sauce.
Serving suggestion: potato gnocchi with chopped hazelnuts.
Recommended drink: a medium red wine.

SLICED BEEF WITH SWEETCORN, BABY ONIONS AND BASMATI RICE

SERVES 4 ■ ■ ■

Preparation and cooking time:
1 hour 20 minutes
Kcal per serving: 665
P = 32g, F = 33g, C = 55g

3 fresh sweetcorn cobs
salt
freshly ground white pepper
30g/1oz butter or margarine
200g/7oz basmati rice
1 tbsp chopped shallots
1–1.25l/1¾–2 pints beef stock
200g/7oz baby onions
400g/14oz beef fillet
2 tbsps grapeseed oil
200ml/7 fl oz double cream
3 tbsps dry sherry
4 tsps sherry vinegar
2 tbsps whipping cream, whipped

Fry the strips of beef until browned.

Fry the sweetcorn kernels and baby onions in the meat juices.

1. Cook the sweetcorn cobs in plenty of salted water for 30–40 minutes or until tender. Scrape off all the kernels with a knife.
2. Melt the butter or margarine in a pan. and gently fry the rice and chopped shallots, stirring constantly, for 5 minutes. Add a little stock, cover and boil gently for 20 minutes, gradually adding more stock as the rice cooks. Depending on the quality of the rice, it will require 500–750ml/18 fl oz-1¼ pints stock.
3. Peel the baby onions, and blanch for 1 minute in lightly salted water. Drain.
4. Pat the beef dry, and cut into thin strips. Season with salt and pepper. Heat the oil in a large pan and fry the beef strips, stirring frequently. Remove from the pan and keep warm. Add the sweetcorn kernels and baby onions to the pan, and gently fry. Season with salt and pepper. Remove from the pan and keep warm.
5. Add 500 ml/18 fl oz of the remaining beef stock, cream, sherry and vinegar to the pan. Bring to the boil and allow to reduce until the sauce becomes creamy. Return the meat and vegetables to the pan, bring to the boil and then fold in the whipped cream.
6. Serve the sliced beef with the rice.
Serving suggestion: fresh green salad.
Recommended drink: a medium rosé wine.

BOILED BEEF IN HORSERADISH AND CAPER SAUCE

SERVES 4 ■

Preparation and cooking time: 15 minutes (not including meat cooking time)
Kcal per serving: 600
P = 20g, F = 56g, C = 3g

300g/10oz boiled beef
500ml/18 fl oz beef stock

FOR THE SAUCE:
2 egg yolks
4 tsps sherry vinegar
1 tsp French mustard
4 tbsps creamed horseradish
125ml/4 fl oz grapeseed oil
salt
freshly ground black pepper
200ml/7 fl oz crème fraîche
150g/5½oz capers

1. Cut the meat into thin slices. Place in a pan with the stock, and warm through.
2. To make the sauce, beat together the egg yolks, vinegar, mustard, horseradish and oil with a hand mixer to make a creamy mayonnaise. Season with salt and pepper, and stir in the crème fraîche and capers.
3. Serve the sauce with the meat.
Serving suggestions: new potatoes and a green salad.
Recommended drink: a dry white wine.

TOP RUMP WITH A MUSHROOM CRUST

SERVES 4 ■ ■

Preparation and cooking time: 40 minutes
Kcal per serving: 445
P = 46g, F = 27g, C = 4g

1 x 600g/1lb 6oz top rump
salt
freshly ground white pepper
3 tbsps grapeseed oil
300g/10oz mushrooms, e.g. shiitake or oyster mushrooms
2 shallots
200g/7oz beef marrow
2 egg yolks
3 tbsps finely chopped fresh parsley
1–2 tbsps breadcrumbs
1 tbsp Dijon mustard

1. Pat the meat dry, and season with salt and pepper. Heat the oil in a flameproof casserole and brown the beef all over. Transfer the casserole to a preheated oven and cook at 200°C/ 400°F/Gas Mark 6 for 15 minutes, turning once.
2. Wipe and chop the mushrooms. Peel and chop the shallots. Cut the marrow into pieces. Place in a pan and warm. Rub through a sieve into a frying pan. Set over a low heat.
3. Gently cook the shallots and mushrooms in the marrow, and season with salt and pepper. Remove the pan from the heat and set aside to cool. Stir the egg yolks and parsley into the mushroom mixture. Add sufficient breadcrumbs to bind and create a workable mixture.
4. Coat the beef with mustard and then with the mushroom mixture. Brown the crust under a preheated grill.
Serving suggestions: gratin dauphinois and shallots with mustard.
Recommended drink: a full-bodied red wine.

VEAL ROLLS

SERVES 4 ■ ■ ■
Preparation and cooking time: 1 hour 10 minutes
Kcal per serving: 745
P = 37g, F = 46g, C = 45g

4 x 120g/5oz veal fillet slices
salt
freshly ground white pepper
bunch of fresh coriander
1 small, ripe mango
60g/2oz butter or margarine
100g/4oz ground cashew nuts
3cm/1in piece root ginger, peeled and grated
1 tsp ground turmeric
125ml/4 fl oz double cream
2 eggs, beaten
200g/7oz desiccated coconut

1. Pat the veal dry, and cut the fillets open lengthways. Place between two sheets of greaseproof paper and pound with a meat hammer. Season with salt and pepper, and sprinkle with a few coriander leaves. Finely chop the remaining leaves.

TIP

Fresh coriander, or Chinese parsley as it is sometimes called, has a strong flavour, so it should be used sparingly. In South America and Asia, it is used in much the same way as we use parsley.

2. Peel the mango, cut the flesh from the stone and dice. Melt 20g/¾oz of the butter or margarine in a flameproof casserole, and gently fry the mango for 2–3 minutes. Add the nuts and ginger, and season with salt, pepper and turmeric. Stir in the cream and bring to the boil. Continue to boil until

Cover the veal fillets first with coriander leaves, then with the mango mixture and finally roll them up tightly.

the liquid has evaporated. Stir in the chopped coriander, remove from the heat and set aside to cool.
3. Spread the mango mixture on the escalopes and roll them up from the short end. Secure with cocktail sticks or trussing thread.
4. Whisk the eggs well. Dip the veal rolls first in the egg and then in the coconut. Press the coconut coating firmly to the rolls.
5. Melt the remaining butter in a flameproof casserole, and fry the veal rolls over a medium heat until they are browned all over. Transfer the casserole to a preheated oven and cook at 200°C/400°F/Gas Mark 6 for 10 minutes.
Serving suggestions: Chinese cabbage and a light sherry sauce with a few pieces of mango and coconut flakes.
Recommended drink: a medium red or white wine.

VEAL ESCALOPES WITH MOZZARELLA CHEESE AND TRUFFLE

SERVES 4 ■ ■
Preparation and cooking time: 30 minutes
Kcal per serving: 445
P = 39g, F = 19g, C = 29g

4 x 120g/5oz veal escalopes
salt
freshly ground white pepper
200g/7oz Mozzarella cheese
1 x 60g/2oz black truffle or truffle trimmings
2 eggs, beaten
200g/7oz breadcrumbs
60g/2oz butter

1. Ask your butcher to cut a 'pocket' in the side of the escalopes, or cut them open and carefully flatten them with the steak hammer. Season with salt and pepper.
2. Cut the Mozzarella cheese and truffle into very thin slices. Stuff these slices into the 'pockets'. Alternatively, sandwich them between the halves of the escalope and secure the edges.
3. Dip the stuffed escalopes first in the egg and then in the breadcrumbs. Press the coating on firmly.
4. Melt the butter in a flameproof casserole, and fry the escalopes on both sides over a medium heat until golden brown. Transfer the casserole to a preheated oven and cook at 200°C/400°F/Gas Mark 6 for 10 minutes.
Serving suggestions: leaf spinach and a light cheese sauce.
Recommended drink: a full-bodied white wine.

SLICES OF VEAL WITH BEANS AND COCONUT

SERVES 4 ■ ■
Preparation and cooking time: 45 minutes
Kcal per serving: 550
P = 26g, F = 39g, C = 24g

400g/14oz veal fillet
300g/10oz broad beans
salt
freshly ground white pepper
3 tbsps grapeseed oil
100g/4oz fresh coconut flakes
milk from 1 coconut
250ml/8 fl oz beef stock
250ml/9 fl oz crème fraîche
1 stalk lemongrass (or a little freshly grated root ginger)
2 tbsps torn basil leaves

1. Pat the veal dry, and cut into thin strips. Shell the broad beans and blanch in boiling salted water for 1 minute. Drain, plunge the beans into cold water and remove the outer green skin.
2. Season the veal with salt and pepper. Heat the oil in a frying pan, and stir-fry the veal for a 5 minutes. Remove from the pan and set aside. Add the beans and coconut flakes to the pan, and fry for 3–4 minutes. Season with salt and pepper. Return the veal to the pan. Add the coconut milk, stock and crème fraîche. Bring to the boil and allow to reduce until creamy.
3. Cut the lemon grass, if using, into thin strips. Stir the lemon grass or ginger and basil into the veal mixture and serve immediately.
Serving suggestion: noodles.
Recommended drink: a medium dry white wine.

LAMB CURRY WITH AUBERGINES, COURGETTES AND TOMATOES

SERVES 4 ■ ■
*Preparation and cooking
time: 40 minutes
Kcal per serving: 440
P = 24g, F = 29g, C = 15g*

2 x 700g/1lb 10oz aubergines
2 x 400g/14oz courgettes
1 onion
400g/14oz lean boneless
    lamb, diced
salt
freshly ground white pepper
1 x 400g/14oz can peeled,
    chopped tomatoes
1 garlic clove
1 red chilli
4 tbsps olive oil
3cm/1in root ginger, peeled
    and grated
2 tsps curry powder
250ml/8 fl oz beef stock
125ml/4 fl oz dry white wine
4 tsps garlic or white wine
    vinegar

1. Wash, trim and dice the aubergines and courgettes. Peel and chop the onion. Season the lamb with salt and pepper.
2. Drain the tomatoes and reserve the juice. Peel and finely chop the garlic. Halve, seed, wash and finely chop the chilli.

*Season the lamb well and then fry
in olive oil.*

*Add the canned tomatoes last,
and season again, if necessary.*

3. Heat the oil in a large flameproof casserole, and fry the lamb, stirring frequently, until browned all over. Add the onions, aubergines and courgettes, and fry, stirring frequently, for 5 minutes. Season with salt and pepper, and stir in the ginger, curry powder, garlic and chilli. Add the reserved tomato juice, stock, wine and vinegar. Cover and simmer for about 10 minutes. Add the tomatoes and adjust the seasoning, if necessary. Heat through and serve.
Serving suggestion: brown or basmati rice or small, fried potatoes.
Recommended drink: a medium dry white wine.

> **TIP**
>
> *The bitter flavour
> of aubergines can
> be alleviated if
> they are sliced,
> sprinkled with
> salt and left to
> drain for 30
> minutes. Rinse,
> pat dry and use
> according to the
> recipe.*

LOIN OF LAMB WITH PISTOU AU GRATIN

(photograph page 68)

SERVES 4 ■ ■
*Preparation and cooking
time: 30 minutes
Kcal per serving: 790
P = 19g, F = 79g, C = 0g*

1 x 600g/1lb 6oz boned loin
    of lamb
salt
freshly ground white pepper
3 tbsps olive oil
2 tbsps Dijon mustard

FOR THE PISTOU:
2 garlic cloves
3 tbsps finely chopped fresh
    parsley
3 tbsps finely chopped fresh
    basil
3 tbsps finely chopped fresh
    chervil
1 tbsp rosemary leaves
1 tbsp thyme leaves
250ml/9 fl oz olive oil
salt
freshly ground white pepper
4–5 tbsps breadcrumbs

1. Wash the lamb and pat dry. Rub salt and pepper into the flesh. Heat the oil in a flameproof casserole, and brown the meat all over. Transfer the casserole to a preheated oven and cook at 200°C/400°F/Gas Mark 6 for 5 minutes.

*To make the pistou, finely chop
the herbs and garlic cloves.*

*Add the oil, breadcrumbs and
seasoning to make a creamy
mixture.*

Coat the lamb first with mustard.

2. Peel and finely chop garlic. Mix together the parsley, basil, chervil, rosemary, thyme, garlic and oil. Season, and gradually add sufficient breadcrumbs to bind the mixture into a workable paste. Remove meat from oven.
3. Coat the lamb surface first with the mustard and then with the pistou. Brown under a preheated grill for a few minutes. Carve at table.
Serving suggestion: potato and courgette fritters.
Recommended drink: a fruity red wine.

> **TIP**
>
> *The loin of lamb
> may be browned
> on the bone. It
> can then be
> boned, and the
> meat can be re-
> arranged on the
> backbone before
> being grilled with
> the pistou
> coating.*

Quick-and-easy Recipes

*M*eat just has to be the ideal ingredient if time is short. When you are in a hurry, you'll be looking for cuts which need only a short cooking time. Liver and chops spring to mind, but shoulder of pork and ribs can also be turned into delicious dishes both quickly and easily. Don't forget minced meat in the race against the clock; escalopes and steaks are also strong candidates in this contest. The lover of fine, fast food may of course be put off by the higher prices of these cuts, but there are many tasty and economical options to choose from as well, and you can still finish with time to spare!

Calf's Liver in Port Cream
(recipe page 84)

BEEF SIRLOIN WITH A PARSLEY CRUST

SERVES 4 ■■
Preparation and cooking time: 30 minutes
Kcal per serving: 470
P = 40g, F = 31g, C = 8g

2 large marrow bones
3 tbsps vegetable oil
750g/1lb 11oz beef sirloin
salt
freshly ground black pepper
4–6 tbsps finely chopped,
  fresh flat-leafed parsley
6 tbsps breadcrumbs
pinch grated nutmeg
pinch cayenne pepper
1 tsp English mustard

1. Place the marrow bones in a bowl and cover with cold water. (This makes the marrow come out more easily.)
2. Heat the oil in a large pan, and fry the beef for about 10 minutes until browned all over. Season, and remove from the pan.
3. To make the herb paste, place the parsley in a bowl with the breadcrumbs. Squeeze the marrow from the bones into the bowl and mash with a fork. Season with salt, pepper, nutmeg and cayenne. Stir in the mustard, and mix thoroughly.
4. Place the beef in an oven-proof dish, and coat the surface with the herb paste. Cook in a preheated oven at 250°C/475°F/Gas Mark 9 for 5–8 minutes, until the crust is golden brown. Extend the cooking time, but lower the oven temperature to 190°C/375F/Gas Mark 5, if you prefer medium rather than rare beef.
5. To serve the meat, cut diagonally into finger-thick slices.
Serving suggestions: mangetout and dauphinois potatoes.
Recommended drink: a robust red wine.

To remove the marrow more easily, soak the bones in cold water.

Fry the sirloin all over until well browned.

Mash the marrow with a fork, and mix well with the parsley, breadcrumbs and spices.

Spread the herb paste over the beef and decorate with a pattern of diagonal lines made with the prongs of a fork.

BEEF FILLET STEAKS WITH CAPER SAUCE

SERVES 4 ■
Preparation and cooking time: 15 minutes
Kcal per serving: 535
P = 38g, F = 40g, C = 2g

3 tbsps vegetable oil
4 x 170g/6oz beef fillet steaks
250ml/9 fl oz dry white wine
4 tbsps capers
200ml/7 fl oz double cream
salt
freshly ground white pepper
pinch cayenne pepper

1. Heat the oil, and fry the steaks over a high heat for 3 minutes on each side. Transfer a dish, cover and keep warm.
2. Pour off the oil. Add the wine to the pan, bring to the boil and allow to reduce by a third.
3. Mix together the capers and cream and stir into the pan. Simmer for a further 3 minutes until creamy. Season with salt, pepper and cayenne pepper.
4. Return the steaks and meat juices to the pan and warm through over a low heat for about 5 minutes.
Serving suggestions: pasta shapes or rice and a tomato salad with basil.
Recommended drink: a light white wine.

RUMP STEAKS WITH A MUSTARD CRUST

SERVES 4 ■■
Preparation and cooking time: 25 minutes
Kcal per serving: 520
P = 38g, F = 40g, C = 2g

75g/3oz sunflower seeds
2 tbsps mustard
2 egg yolks
salt
freshly ground black pepper
½ tsp sweet paprika
4 x 180g/6oz rump steaks
3 tbsps vegetable oil

1. Crush the sunflower seeds finely in a grinder or with a pestle in a mortar.
2. Beat together the mustard and egg yolks, and stir in the ground sunflower seeds. Season with salt, pepper and paprika.
3. Trim the steaks and pat dry. Heat the oil, and fry the steaks over a high heat for 2–3 minutes on each side.
4. Remove the steaks from the pan and place them on a baking tray lined with aluminium foil. Spread the mustard paste evenly on top. Bake in a preheated oven at 250°C/475°F/Gas Mark 9 or cook under a preheated grill for 3–5 minutes until golden brown.
Serving suggestions: potato pancakes and tomato salad with spring onions, broccoli in cream.
Recommended drink: beer.

> **TIP**
>
> *For a hot crust use Dijon mustard.*

STUFFED ROLLS OF VEAL WITH BASIL

SERVES 4 ■ ■
Preparation and cooking time: 35 minutes
Kcal per serving: 400
P = 42g, F = 19g, C = 6g

3 bunches basil
2 tbsps breadcrumbs
2 egg yolks
salt
freshly ground black pepper
3 tbsps olive oil
4 x 180g/6oz thin veal
  escalopes
2 onions
250ml/8 fl oz dry white wine
3 tbsps crème fraîche
dash lemon juice
dash Worcestershire sauce

Rinse the basil, shake dry and chop finely.

Season the veal escalopes, coat with the herb mixture, roll up and secure with cocktail sticks.

Beat the crème fraîche into the cooking liquid, season and add the lemon juice and Worcestershire sauce.

1. Rinse the basil and shake dry. Pick off the leaves and reserve a few of the best for the garnish. Finely chop the remaining leaves.
2. Mix together the breadcrumbs and egg yolks, and season with salt and pepper. Add 1 tbsp of the olive oil and stir well to make a smooth mixture.
3. Pound the veal escalopes with a steak hammer. Pat dry and season both sides with salt and pepper. Spread the breadcrumb mixture on the escalopes, roll up tightly and secure with cocktail sticks or trussing thread.
4. Peel and finely chop the onions. Heat the remaining oil in a large frying pan, and gently fry the veal rolls until browned all over. Add the onions, and fry until transparent. Pour in the white wine, cover and cook for 20 minutes.
5. Remove the rolls from the pan. Beat the crème fraîche into the cooking liquid, bring to the boil and season with salt and pepper. Add the lemon juice and Worcestershire sauce.
6. Serve the veal rolls with the sauce on warmed plates, and garnish with the reserved basil leaves.
Other herbs may be used for the filling and ground almonds are an alternative to breadcrumbs.
Serving suggestions: potato fritters and a salad with cherry tomatoes.
Recommended drink: a hearty Italian red wine.

CALF'S LIVER IN PORT WINE CREAM SAUCE

(photograph page 80)

SERVES 4 ■
Preparation and cooking time: 25 minutes
Kcal per serving: 695
P = 37g, F = 44g, C = 23g

750g/1lb 11oz calf's liver
3 shallots
2 tbsps flour
40g/1½oz butter
250ml/8 fl oz port
250ml/9 fl oz double cream
salt
freshly ground white pepper
½ tsp dried marjoram
2 tsps lemon juice
bunch of chervil

1. Place the calf's liver in tepid water for 2–3 minutes. Then pull off the skin and cut into finger-thick slices. Peel and finely chop the shallots.
2. Sift the flour onto a plate and coat the liver slices.
3. Melt the butter in a large frying pan, and fry the strips of liver, in batches if necessary, until browned all over. Remove, cover and set aside.
4. Gently fry the shallots in the same pan until transparent. Add the port, bring to the boil and allow to reduce by half.
5. Stir in the cream, and simmer gently for about 8 minutes until the sauce is creamy. Season with salt and pepper, and stir in the marjoram and lemon juice.
6. Return the strips of liver to the pan and warm through for 2–3 minutes.
7. Meanwhile, rinse and dry the chervil. Remove the stalks and stir the leaves into the sauce before serving.
Serving suggestion: mashed potato.
Recommended drink: a light, dry white wine.

ESCALOPES OF VEAL WITH GRAPEFRUIT

SERVES 4 ■ ■
Preparation and cooking time: 30 minutes
Kcal per serving: 320
P = 37g, F = 12g, C = 15g

4 x 180g/6oz veal escalopes
30g/1oz butter
1 tbsp oil
salt
freshly ground white pepper
½ tsp grated nutmeg
2 grapefruit, preferably pink
4 tsps Cointreau
1 tbsp chopped pistachio nuts

1. Make a deep cut in the side of the veal escalopes, open them out and flatten with a steak hammer. Pat dry.
2. Heat the butter and oil in a large frying pan, and fry the escalopes over a high heat for 1 minute on each side. Season with salt, pepper and a little nutmeg. Remove from the pan, cover and set aside.
3. Squeeze the juice from one grapefruit and mix together with the Cointreau. Pour into the pan and allow to reduce by a third over a gentle heat.
4. Meanwhile, peel the second grapefruit and remove the white pith and inner skin. With a sharp knife, cut the flesh into segments.
5. Season the sauce with salt, pepper and a little nutmeg. Return the meat and meat juices to the pan and warm through.
6. Arrange the grapefruit segments on 4 plates, place the veal escalopes beside them and sprinkle over the pistachio nuts.
Serving suggestions: rice and salad.
Recommended drink: a light, dry white wine.

PORK FILLET WITH HERB SAUCE

SERVES 4 ◼
*Preparation and cooking
time: 30 minutes
Kcal per serving: 500
P = 42g, F = 36g, C = 2g*

750g/1lb 11oz pork fillet
3 tbsps oil
salt
freshly ground black pepper
pinch freshly grated nutmeg
200ml/6 fl oz meat stock
200g/7oz cream cheese with
　herbs
2 garlic cloves
dash lemon juice
3 tbsps finely chopped fresh
　mixed herbs

Finely chopped fresh herbs give the sauce extra flavour.

Brown the beef fillet all over in hot oil.

Add the cream cheese to the sauce allowing plenty of time for it to melt.

1. Trim the pork, rinse and pat dry. Heat the oil in a large frying pan and fry the pork until browned all over. Season with salt, pepper and a little nutmeg. Cover and cook for 15 minutes.
2. Remove the pork from the pan, cover and set aside. Pour off the fat. Add the stock to the pan over a low heat, scraping the base of the pan to deglaze.
3. Add the cream cheese, stirring constantly until it has melted. Peel and crush the garlic and add to the sauce. Simmer for about 3 minutes. Season with salt, pepper and lemon juice. Stir in the herbs.
4. Return the pork and the meat juices to the pan, and simmer again for a further 3 minutes.
5. Cut the fillet into 5mm/¼-inch slices and arrange in a fan-shaped pattern on 4 plates. Pour over the herb sauce.
Serving suggestion: baked potatoes.
Recommended drink: a light white wine.

Finally, stir the herbs and spices into the cheese sauce.

CURRIED PORK WITH TOMATOES

SERVES 4 ◼
*Preparation and cooking
time: 30 minutes
Kcal per serving: 655
P = 34g, F = 54g, C = 8g*

750g/1lb 11oz boneless
　shoulder of pork
1 large onion
3 tbsps oil
2 tbsps curry powder
salt
freshly ground black pepper
2 x 400g/14oz cans tomatoes
1 bay leaf
½ bunch spring onions

1. Cut the pork into 1cm/½-inch cubes. Peel and finely chop the onion. Heat the oil in a large frying pan, and fry the pork over a high heat until browned all over.
2. Add the onion and curry powder, and gently fry for a further 5 minutes. Season with salt and pepper.
3. Add the tomatoes, can juice and bay leaf. Bring to the boil, cover and simmer for 20 minutes.
4. Meanwhile, wash and trim the spring onions. Slice into thin rings.
5. Taste the curry and, if necessary, add a little more seasoning.
Serving suggestion: buttered rice with flaked almonds and a green salad with a herb vinaigrette.
Recommended drink: a dry rosé wine.

ESCALOPE OF PORK WITH TUNA FISH SAUCE

SERVES 4 ◼◼
*Preparation and cooking
time: 30 minutes
Kcal per serving: 655
P = 50g, F = 47g, C = 3g*

40g/1½oz butter
4 pork escalopes
salt
freshly ground white pepper
125ml/4 fl oz dry white wine
1 x 200g/7oz can of tuna fish
200ml/7 fl oz double cream
3 anchovy fillets, soaked
2 tsps balsamic vinegar
juice of ½ lime
2 tbsps finely chopped chervil

1. Melt the butter in a frying pan, and fry the meat for 3

Purée the sauce with a hand-held mixer.

minutes on each side. Remove from the pan, season, set aside and keep warm.
2. Pour off the fat. Add the wine to the pan over a low heat, scraping the base of the pan to deglaze.
3. Drain the tuna. Add to the pan and break it up with a fork. Stir in the cream and bring to the boil. Finely chop the anchovy fillets and add.
4. Purée the sauce with a hand-held mixer, and heat through. Season, and stir in the vinegar and lime juice.
5. Place the escalopes on 4 plates, pour over the sauce and sprinkle with chervil.
Serving suggestion: baguette.

PORK ESCALOPE WITH MOZZARELLA

SERVES 4
Preparation and cooking time: 20 minutes
Kcal per serving: 480
P = 47g, F = 32g, C = 1g

Heat the butter and olive oil.

30g/1oz butter
2 tbsps olive oil
4 x 180g/6oz pork escalopes
salt
freshly ground black pepper
4 garlic cloves
½ bunch basil
150g/5½oz Mozzarella cheese

1. Heat the butter and olive oil in a large frying pan. Pat the pork dry, and fry for 2 minutes on each side. Season with salt and pepper.
2. Arrange the escalopes side by side in an ovenproof dish or on a baking tray.
3. Peel and crush the garlic. Spread the crushed garlic on the pork. Rinse the basil and shake dry. Pick the leaves from the stalks and sprinkle over the meat, reserving a few leaves for the garnish. Cut the Mozzarella cheese into 8 slices. Top each escalope with 2 slices of cheese. Season with salt and pepper, and drizzle over the olive oil.
4. Bake in a preheated oven at 250°C/475°F/Gas Mark 9 until the cheese begins to melt. Remove from the oven and transfer to a serving dish. Garnish with the reserved basil leaves.
Serving suggestions: rocket and cherry tomato salad with warm white bread.
Recommended drink: a fresh, light white wine.

Season the escalopes with salt and pepper and spread with crushed garlic.

Cut the Mozzarella cheese into 8 slices.

Cover the pork escalopes first with basil and then Mozzarella.

HOT SPICED PORK WITH SWEETCORN

SERVES 4
Preparation and cooking time: 35 minutes
Kcal per serving: 395
P = 28g, F = 21g, C = 22g

600g/1lb 6oz pork spare rib
3 tbsps oil
3 garlic cloves
1 large onion
2 green or red chillies
1 x 500g/1lb 2oz can chopped tomatoes
1 x 280g/9oz can sweetcorn
thyme sprig
salt
freshly ground black pepper

1. Rinse the pork and pat dry. Cut into 15mm/¾-inch cubes. Heat the oil, and fry the pork, in batches, until brown.
2. Peel and crush the garlic. Peel and chop the onion. Add the garlic and onion to the pan, and fry for a further 5 minutes.
3. Halve, seed and wash the chillies. Cut into thin rings and add to the pan. Stir in the tomatoes with their can juice. Cover and cook for 10 minutes.
4. Drain the sweetcorn. Stir the sweetcorn and thyme into the pan, cover and cook for a further 10 minutes.
5. Season with salt and pepper. Remove and discard thyme before serving.
Serving suggestions: buttered rice with chopped green pistachios and a mixed green salad with a yogurt dressing.
Recommended drink: beer or red wine.

PORK CHOPS IN RED WINE SAUCE

SERVES 4
Preparation and cooking time: 20 minutes
Kcal per serving: 525
P = 31g, F = 35g, C = 5g

4 x 150g/5½oz pork chops, trimmed of excess fat
3 tbsps oil
salt
freshly ground black pepper
1 large onion
60g/2oz smoked, streaky bacon, rinded
2 tsps flour
375ml/14 fl oz dry red wine
1 tsp dried marjoram

1. Pat the chops dry. Heat the oil in a pan, and fry the chops for 4 minutes on each side. Season with salt and pepper, remove from the pan, cover and set aside.
2. Peel and finely chop the onion. Fry the onion in the same pan until transparent.
3. Dice the bacon. Add the bacon to the pan, and fry for 5 minutes over a medium heat.
4. Sprinkle with the flour, and cook, stirring constantly, for 2 minutes. Stir in the wine. Sprinkle over the marjoram, and simmer for a further 5 minutes. Season with salt and pepper. Return the chops and their juices to the pan and warm through in the sauce.
5. Arrange the pork chops with the sauce on warm plates.
Serving suggestion: mashed potato.
Recommended drink: a dry red wine.

ESCALOPE OF PORK IN PARMESAN CHEESE

SERVES 4 ■■
Preparation and cooking time: 25 minutes
Kcal per serving: 485
P = 46g, F = 31g, C = 6g

4 tbsps breadcrumbs
4 tbsps grated Parmesan
  cheese
1 egg
4 x 180g/6oz thin pork
  escalopes
salt
freshly ground black pepper
2 garlic cloves
3 tbsps sunflower oil
1 lemon

Coat the pork escalopes in the breadcrumb and cheese mixture.

1. Mix together the bread-crumbs and Parmesan cheese in a shallow bowl. Beat the egg in another shallow bowl.
2. Flatten the pork escalopes with a steak hammer, and pat dry. Cut each escalope in half.
3. Season the meat with salt and pepper, and then dip the slices first in the beaten egg and then in the bread-crumb and cheese mixture. Press the coating firmly in place.
4. Peel and quarter the garlic cloves. Heat the oil in a pan, fry the garlic until brown. Remove from the pan and discard. Fry the escalopes in the garlic oil over a medium heat for 3 minutes on each side.
5. Cut the lemon into 8. Transfer the escalopes to a serving dish and garnish with the lemon.
Cheese-coated pork escalopes can be eaten hot or cold.
Serving suggestion: potato and cucumber salad or steamed Swiss chard with mashed potatoes.
Recommended drink: a dry rosé wine.

Quarter the garlic cloves and fry them in oil until golden brown.

Fry the breaded escalopes in the garlic oil for a total of 6 minutes.

PORK CHOPS STUFFED WITH FETA CHEESE

SERVES 4 ■■
Preparation and cooking time: 30 minutes
Kcal per serving: 440
P = 32g, F = 34g, C = 2g

100g/4oz Feta cheese
60g/2oz stoned green olives
1 garlic clove
salt
freshly ground black pepper
4 x 200g/7oz pork chops
3 tbsps vegetable oil
1 lemon

1. Mash the Feta cheese with a fork.
2. Coarsely chop the olives and mix with the cheese. Peel and crush the garlic and combine with the cheese and olives. Season with salt and pepper.
3. Cut a slit in the side of the pork chops and stuff each 'pocket' with the cheese mixture. Sew up the opening with trussing thread.
4. Heat the oil in a large frying pan, and fry the chops for about 4 minutes on each side. Season with salt and pepper.
5. Quarter the lemon and serve the segments with the pork chops.
If preferred, chopped onion and a few mixed herbs may be added to the Feta cheese mixture.
Serving suggestions: roast potatoes or sesame seed rolls and a cucumber salad with onion, dill and yogurt dressing.
Recommended drink: a dry white wine.

Mash the Feta cheese with a fork.

Coarsely chop the olives with a sharp knife.

Spoon the seasoned cheese mixture into the 'pockets'.

Sew up the openings with trussing thread.

90

LAMB RAGOÛT WITH ALMONDS AND MINT

SERVES 4 ■
Preparation and cooking time: 30 minutes
Kcal per serving: 840
P = 39g, F = 73g, C = 7g

750g/1lb 11oz leg or loin of
 lamb
1 large onion
40g/1½oz butter
juice and peel of 1 lemon
150g/5½oz ground almonds
200ml/7 fl oz double cream
250ml/8 fl oz lamb stock
salt
freshly ground white pepper
pinch ground cumin
1 tsp chopped root ginger
bunch of fresh mint

1. Rinse the lamb and pat dry. Cut into slices and then into strips. Peel and finely chop the onion. Melt the butter in a large frying pan, and fry the lamb strips, in batches if necessary, until browned all over. Remove from the pan, cover and set aside.
2. Fry the onion in the same pan. Add the lemon juice and peel, and bring to the boil. Stir in the almonds, and cook for a further 3 minutes. Add the cream and stock, and bring to the boil.
3. Return the meat to the pan. Season with salt, pepper, cumin and ginger, and simmer for 15 minutes.
4. Meanwhile, rinse the mint and shake dry. Tear off the leaves and mix with the lamb.
Serving suggestions: curried rice with raisins and a green salad.
Recommended drink: a hearty red wine.

LAMB CUTLETS WITH CUCUMBER

SERVES 4 ■
Preparation and cooking time: 25 minutes
Kcal per serving: 745
P = 23g, F = 71g, C = 3g

1 large cucumber
30g/1oz butter
2 garlic cloves
salt
freshly ground white pepper
6 tbsps crème fraîche
3 tbsps finely chopped fresh
 dill
3 tbsps olive oil
8 x 80g/3oz lamb cutlets
2 tsps finely chopped
 rosemary

1. Peel the cucumber, cut in half lengthways and scrape out the seeds with a spoon. Cut the halves into very thin slices.
2. Melt the butter in a pan, and gently fry the cucumber for about 5 minutes. Peel and chop the garlic. Add the garlic to the pan, and stir well. Season with salt and pepper. Stir in the crème fraîche, and cook for a further 5 minutes. Stir in the dill.
3. Heat the oil in a large frying pan, and fry the lamb cutlets for 2–3 minutes on each side. After turning the meat, season with salt and pepper and sprinkle with the rosemary.
4. Transfer the cutlets to a warm serving dish, arrange the cucumber around them and serve.
Serving suggestion: small, roast potatoes or sesame seed rolls.
Recommended drink: retsina or another Greek white wine.

Peel the cucumber, cut in half lengthways and slice thinly.

Season the cucumber with salt and pepper, add two crushed garlic cloves and the crème fraîche, and cook for 5 minutes.

Add finely chopped dill to the cucumber.

Brown the lamb cutlets in olive oil. Season with salt, pepper and rosemary.

LAMB AND RED PEPPERS

SERVES 4 ■
Preparation and cooking time: 25 minutes
Kcal per serving: 530
P = 28g, F = 44g, C = 4g

600g/1lb 6oz leg or loin of
 lamb
3 tbsps olive oil
1 large onion
3 garlic cloves
1 x 200g/7oz jar of skinned
 red peppers
salt
freshly ground black pepper
pinch cayenne pepper
1 tsp sweet paprika
3 tbsps tomato purée
4 tbsps crème fraîche
juice of ½ lemon
3 tbsps finely chopped flat-
 leafed parsley
parsley leaves to garnish
 (optional)

1. Rinse the lamb and pat dry. Cut into slices and then into finger-thick strips.
2. Heat the olive oil in a large saucepan, and fry the meat, in batches if necessary, until browned all over.
3. Peel and finely chop the onion. Peel and crush the garlic. Add the onion and garlic to the pan, and fry for a further 5 minutes.
4. Drain the red peppers and cut them into matchstick strips. Stir the peppers into the pan, and season with salt, pepper, cayenne pepper and paprika. Stir in the tomato purée, crème fraîche and lemon juice, lower the heat and simmer gently for 10 minutes.
5. Stir in the chopped parsley. If liked, garnish with a few flat-leafed parsley leaves before serving.
Serving suggestion: croquette potatoes.
Recommended drink: a hearty red wine.

Microwave Recipes

*N*ew recipes have been developed that ensure that meat cooked in the microwave oven is not tough or dry. Those home cooks with combination ovens will certainly derive the greatest benefit from this quick way of cooking meat. Joints and fillets can be cooked in a basic microwave, but the heat of a conventional oven or a grill is necessary for a well-browned finish. Whichever method is chosen, remember that special microwave-safe cooking utensils are essential! Whatever the cut of meat, modern kitchen technology ensures that the cooked meat is tender and retains its natural flavour. Use salt sparingly, replacing it with the herbs and spices which will enhance the natural flavours. All recipes are for a standard 600 watt microwave, except where a combination microwave oven is specified.

Veal in Curry Sauce
(recipe page 99)

BOILED BEEF WITH SPRING VEGETABLES

SERVES 2
Standard microwave oven
Preparation and cooking
time: 45 minutes
Kcal per serving: 435
P = 46g, F = 21g, C = 15g

500ml/18 fl oz water
1 x 500g/1lb 2oz T-bone steak
salt
freshly ground black pepper
4 carrots, preferably with
    tops
4 spring onions
2 sticks celery
100g/4oz mangetout
1 tbsp chopped fresh parsley

Place the seasoned joint in the hot water.

1. Pour the water into a microwave-safe dish large enough to take the meat and vegetables. Heat the water on *HIGH* for 3–4 minutes. Season the meat with salt and pepper. Place the steak in the hot water and cook on *HIGH* for 15 minutes.

Arrange the vegetables around the beef and baste with the cooking liquid.

TIP

The meat must have been well hung; the flesh should be deep red in colour. If not, allow more time before adding the vegetables.

---

2. Meanwhile, peel the carrots, but leave a short length of the green tops. Trim the spring onions and remove the last third of the green leaves. Trim and wash the celery and cut into matchstick strips. Trim the mangetout.
3. Turn the meat over. Arrange the carrots, onions and celery around the sides, season with salt and baste with a little of the cooking

Miniature corn cobs could be added to the mangetout.

liquid. Cover and cook on *HIGH* for 8–10 minutes. Add the mangetout, and cook on *HIGH* for a further 5 minutes.
4. Leave the meat to stand for a few minutes, sprinkle with parsley and serve in the dish.
Serving suggestion: boiled potatoes.
Recommended drink: a medium white wine.

MEATBALLS IN PAPRIKA SAUCE

SERVES 4
Standard microwave oven
Preparation and cooking
time: 40 minutes
Kcal per serving: 370
P = 26g, F = 22g, C = 16g

1 onion
2 garlic cloves
3 tbsps vegetable oil
1 small red pepper
1 small yellow pepper
1 small green pepper
3 beefsteak tomatoes
salt
freshly ground black pepper
1 tbsp sweet paprika
1 thyme sprig
1 rosemary sprig
125ml/4 fl oz meat stock
1 bread roll or thick slice
    white bread
1 egg
1 tbsp chopped fresh parsley
350g/11oz minced beef
1 tsp English made mustard

The best time of year for peppers is from August to October.

1. Peel and chop the onion and garlic. Place the onion, garlic and oil in a microwave-safe dish, and cook on *HIGH* for 3–4 minutes until transparent. Reserve 2 tbsps of the onion mixture.
2. Halve, seed, wash and dice the peppers. Cut crosses in the tomato skins, dip in water, cover and cook on *HIGH* for 3–4 minutes. Rinse and skin. Quarter, seed and dice.
3. Stir the peppers and tomatoes into the onions, and season with salt, pepper and paprika. Add the herbs and stock, cover and cook on *HIGH* for 10–12 minutes.
4. To prepare the meatballs, place the roll or bread in a bowl, cover with lukewarm water and set aside to soak. Mix together the reserved onions, egg, parsley and minced beef. Squeeze the water from the roll or bread, and add to the meatball mixture. Knead thoroughly to make a smooth workable

Pour stock over the chopped, seasoned vegetables, cover and cook.

mixture. Season with salt, pepper and add the mustard.
5. Shape the mixture into 12 meatballs, and place in the pepper sauce. Cover and cook on *HIGH* for 3–5 minutes. Leave to stand for a few minutes. If required sprinkle with parsley.
Serving suggestions: penne or other large pasta shapes and a salad.
Recommended drink: a light Italian red wine.

VEAL SWEETBREADS IN VEGETABLES

SERVES 2 ■■

*Standard microwave oven
Preparation and cooking
time: 35 minutes
Resting time: 2 hours
Kcal per serving: 415
P = 31g, F = 23g, C = 12g*

*300g/10oz calf's sweetbreads
2 spring onions
2 carrots
2 sticks celery
100g/4oz mushrooms
40g/1½oz butter
125ml/4 fl oz veal stock
125ml/4 fl oz dry white wine
salt
freshly ground white pepper
1 tbsp chopped fresh herbs*

1. Place the sweetbreads in a bowl and cover with cold water. Set aside to soak, changing the water frequently until the water remains clear and the sweetbreads are white. Drain and trim.
2. Trim and wash the spring onions and cut into matchstick strips. Peel the carrots and cuts into matchstick strips. Trim and wash the celery and cut into matchstick strips. Wipe and slice the mushrooms.
3. Place the butter in a microwave-safe dish and melt on *HIGH for 2–3 minutes*. Stir the onions, carrots, celery and mushrooms into the butter, cover and cook on *HIGH for 3–4 minutes*.
4. Add the wine and stock, and season with salt and pepper. Cover and cook on *HIGH for 4–5 minutes*.
5. Add sweetbreads, and spoon over some vegetables. Cook on *MEDIUM for 5–6 minutes*. Leave to stand for a few minutes. Sprinkle with the herbs and serve.
Serving suggestion: boiled potatoes.
Recommended drink: a fruity red wine.

VEAL IN CURRY SAUCE

(photograph page 94)

SERVES 4 ■

*Standard microwave oven
Preparation and cooking
time: 30 minutes
Marinate for 1 hour
Kcal per serving: 320
P = 23g, F = 19g, C = 5g*

*400g/14oz silverside of veal
5mm/½-inch piece root ginger
1 small piece of dried chilli
2 tbsps soy sauce
4 tbsps rice wine or dry
 sherry
1 leek
200g/7oz mushrooms
3 tbsps oil
125ml/5 fl oz cream
1 tbsp mild curry powder
salt
freshly ground white pepper
1 tsp cornflour
4 tbsps chicken stock
coriander leaves (optional)*

1. Rinse the veal and pat dry. Cut into thin strips and place in a bowl. Finely grate the ginger and crush the chilli. Mix together the ginger, chilli, soy sauce and rice wine or sherry. Pour over the veal strips and stir well. Cover and set aside to marinate for about an hour.
2. Meanwhile, trim and wash the leek and cut into matchstick strips. Wipe and thinly slice the mushrooms.
3. Mix together the oil, leek and mushrooms in a large microwave-safe dish and cook on *HIGH for 5–6 minutes*, stirring frequently.
4. Add the veal, marinade and cream. Stir in the curry powder, and season with salt and pepper. Stir thoroughly. Cover and cook on *HIGH for 5–6 minutes*.
5. Stir the cornflour into the chicken stock to make a smooth paste. Stir the paste into the veal and vegetable mixture. Cook on *HIGH for 3–4 minutes*. If liked, sprinkle

Mix together the grated ginger, chilli, soy sauce and sherry. Marinate the veal strips in the mixture.

Sprinkle the veal with curry powder.

with coriander leaves. Soya bean sprouts or a few mangetout can be included in the vegetable mixture.
Serving suggestion: fluffy rice.
Recommended drink: a fruity Italian white wine.

VEAL RAGOÛT WITH ANCHOVIES

SERVES 4 ■

*Standard microwave oven
Preparation and cooking
time: 40 minutes
Kcal per serving: 235
P = 24g, F = 12g, C = 7g*

*400g/14oz silverside of veal
1 large onion
3 sticks celery
2 small courgettes
3 beefsteak tomatoes
3–4 chopped anchovies
1 small piece of dried chilli
salt
freshly ground white pepper
1 tsp sweet paprika
4 tbsps olive oil
juice of 1 lemon*

1. Rinse the veal and pat dry. Cut into 15mm/¾-inch cubes. Peel and chop the onion. Trim and chop the celery and courgettes. Blanch, skin, seed and chop the beafsteak tomatoes.
2. Chop the anchovies. Mix together the chilli, anchovies, veal, onion, celery, courgettes and tomatoes in a large microwave-safe dish. Season with salt, pepper and paprika. Add the oil and lemon juice, cover and cook on *HIGH for 18–20 minutes*. Stir well before serving.
Serving suggestion: noodles.
Recommended drink: a Spanish rosé.

> **TIP**
>
> *This ragoût is ideal for hot summer days as it also tastes delicious cold.*

STUFFED BREAST OF PORK WITH PRUNES AND WALNUTS

SERVES 8 ■ ■
*Combination microwave
oven
Preparation and cooking
time: 1 hour 40 minutes
Kcal per serving: 415
P = 45g, F = 14g, C = 19g*

2kgs/4½lbs breast of pork
salt
freshly ground black pepper

FOR THE STUFFING:
3 day-old bread rolls
250ml/9 fl oz milk
100g/4oz prunes, stoned
125ml/4 fl oz brandy
2 egg yolks
salt
freshly ground black pepper
pinch ground cinnamon
grated peel of ½ orange
60g/2oz walnuts, chopped
1 tbsp chopped parsley
1–2 tbsps breadcrumbs

TO SERVE:
250ml/9 fl oz meat stock
2 tbsps crème fraîche

1. Ask your butcher to cut a 'pocket' in the breast of pork. Rinse the meat, pat dry and rub salt and pepper into the flesh, including inside the 'pocket'.
2. To make the stuffing, cut the rolls into slices. Warm the milk on *HIGH for 1–2 minutes*, and pour over the bread. Chop the prunes and place in a microwave-safe dish. Pour over the brandy and cook on *MEDIUM for 2–3 minutes*. Drain the prunes and reserve the brandy.
3. Squeeze the milk from the bread. Work the bread to a smooth paste in a blender with half the prunes. Add the remaining prunes and the egg yolks, and season with salt and pepper. Stir in the cinnamon, orange peel, walnuts and parsley and, if the

Squeeze the milk from the rolls and purée them with half the drained prunes.

mixture is too soft, add a few breadcrumbs.
4. Reserve a little stuffing and spoon the remainder into the breast of pork. Secure the opening with trussing thread and place in an ovenproof, microwave-safe dish. Place the reserved stuffing alongside and cook on *MEDIUM for 15 minutes* in a combination microwave preheated to 220°C/425°F (fan-assisted 200°C/400°F). Add the stock and reserved brandy and cook on *LOW for 40–45 minutes* at 200°C/400°F (fan-assisted 180°C/350°F).
5. Remove the pork, cover with aluminium foil and leave to rest. Stir the crème fraîche into the sauce, reduce on *HIGH for 5 minutes*. Rub the sauce through a sieve.
6. Cut the pork into slices with a sharp knife. Serve the sauce separately.
Serving suggestions: dumplings and broccoli.
Recommended drink: a full-bodied red wine.

FILLET OF PORK WITH GORGONZOLA SAUCE

SERVES 2 ■
*Combination microwave
oven
Preparation and cooking
time: 20 minutes
Kcal per serving: 595
P = 39g, F = 45g, C = 2g*

1 x 300g/10oz pork fillet
salt
freshly ground black pepper
2 shallots
1 tbsp vegetable oil
15g/½oz butter
4 tsps dry sherry
1 tsp sherry vinegar
100g/4oz Gorgonzola cheese
3 tbsps double cream
1 tbsp chopped fresh parsley

1. Rinse the pork and pat dry. Rub salt and pepper into the flesh. Peel and chop the shallots.
2. Place the oil, butter and shallots in a microwave-safe dish and cook on *HIGH for 3–4 minutes* until transparent. Coat the pork with the melted butter and shallots, and pour over the sherry and vinegar. Cover the dish and cook on *HIGH for 3–4 minutes*.
3. Purée the cream and cheese in a blender. Coat the pork with the Gorgonzola cream.
4. Switch on the grill and cook on *HIGH for 4–5 minutes*. Leave to stand for a few minutes and then sprinkle with parsley.
If the sauce is too thin, reduce it by boiling for *a few minutes on HIGH*. In the meantime, keep the meat warm.
Serving suggestions: tagliatelle and young French beans.
Recommended drink: a dry white wine.

ROAST PORK WITH HERBS

SERVES 6–8 ■
*Combination microwave
oven
Preparation and cooking
time: 1¼ hours
Kcal per serving if serving 6:
410
P = 38g, F = 26g, C = 1g*

1.5kgs/3¼lbs loin of pork with bones
2 thyme sprigs
1 oregano sprig
2 basil sprigs
3 sage leaves
2 tarragon leaves
bunch of parsley
2 garlic cloves
1 onion
2 tbsps herb mustard
salt
freshly ground black pepper
125ml/4 fl oz dry white wine

1. Ask your butcher to remove the flesh from the backbone but keep the bones.
2. Chop the thyme, oregano, basil, sage, tarragon and parsley. Peel and chop the garlic and onion. Mix together the chopped herbs, garlic, onion and mustard.
3. Rinse the pork and pat dry. Rub salt and pepper into the flesh, and coat with the herb paste. Place the meat on its backbone. Cook on a roasting tray with a drip pan underneath on *LOW for 50–55 minutes* in a combination microwave preheated to 200°C/400°F (fan-assisted 180°C/350°F) until crisp.
4. Remove the pork, cover and leave to stand. Add the white wine to the meat juices and cook on *HIGH for 4–5 minutes*.
5. Cut the pork into slices and serve the wine and herb sauce separately.
Serving suggestion: grilled potatoes with soured cream.
Recommended drink: a chilled beer.

SHOULDER OF SUCKLING PIG WITH HONEY AND APRICOT SAUCE

Brush the top surface of the seasoned meat with the mustard and honey mixture.

SERVES 6 ■
*Combination microwave oven
Preparation and cooking time: 1 hour 20 minutes
Kcal per serving: 740
P = 44g, F = 57g, C = 10g*

*2kgs/4½lbs suckling pig
salt
freshly ground black pepper
6–8 cloves
1 tbsp English mustard
2 tbsps clear honey
grated peel of ½ orange
1 tsp grated root ginger
½ tsp ground cinnamon
pinch cayenne pepper
125ml/4 fl oz white wine
125ml/4 fl oz veal stock
250g/8oz apricots*

1. Ask your butcher to score a diamond pattern in the pork rind. Wash the meat and pat dry. Rub the flesh with salt and pepper. Stud the pork with cloves and place in a large, ovenproof microwave-safe dish.
2. Stir together the mustard, honey, orange peel, ginger, cinnamon and cayenne pepper, and season with salt and pepper. Brush the mixture over the pork rind. Combine the remainder with the wine and stock.
3. Cook the shoulder, with the rind facing down, on *MEDIUM for 20 minutes* in a combination microwave preheated to 200°C/400°F (fan-assisted 180°C/350°F).
4. Meanwhile, wash, halve and stone the apricots.
5. Turn the shoulder over, arrange the apricots around the joint and pour over half the wine and honey mixture. Cook for a further *20 minutes on MEDIUM* at 180°C/350°F (fan-assisted 160°C/325°F). Baste the

Pour the wine and honey mixture over the pork shoulder and apricots.

shoulder with the remaining wine and honey mixture and cook on the same setting for a further 10 minutes.
6. Remove the meat, cover with aluminium foil and keep warm. Strain the sauce through a sieve. Cut the joint into slices and hand the sauce separately.
Serving suggestions: boiled potatoes and Brussels sprouts.
Recommended drink: a fruity white wine.

ROAST PORK WITH ORANGE AND RAISIN SAUCE

Brush the meat with the orange marinade and leave for a few hours.

SERVES 4 ■
*Combination microwave oven
Preparation and cooking time: 1 hour
Marinate for several hours
Kcal per serving: 555
P = 38g, F = 31g, C = 21g*

*800g/1¾lbs boneless neck of pork
salt
freshly ground white pepper
1 tsp chopped fresh rosemary
2 tbsps orange marmalade
grated rind of 1 orange
1 tbsp English mustard
5 tbsps medium dry sherry
60g/2oz raisins
juice of 1–2 oranges*

1. Rinse the pork and pat dry. Rub salt and pepper into the flesh. Mix together the rosemary, marmalade, orange peel, mustard and half the sherry. Place the pork in an ovenproof, microwave-safe dish. Brush the surface with the marinade, cover with aluminium foil and leave in the refrigerator to marinate for a few hours.

> **TIP**
>
> *To boost the orange flavour, add a few orange segments to the juice.*

2. Place the raisins in a microwave-safe dish and cover with the remaining sherry. Cook on *MEDIUM for 3–4 minutes.* Cover and leave to stand.
3. Cook the pork on *MEDIUM for 10 minutes* in a combination microwave preheated to 200°C/400°F (fan-assisted 180°C/350°F) . Add

After about 10 minutes, add the orange juice to the dish.

the orange juice to the meat juices, and cook on the same settings for a further 10 minutes. Add the soaked raisins and sherry, and cook on the same settings for a further 15–20 minutes until brown and crisp.
4. Remove the meat from the oven, cover with aluminium foil and leave to stand. If necessary, reduce the sauce by boiling *on HIGH for 2–3 minutes.*
5. Cut the pork into thin slices and pour over the sauce.
This joint tastes delicious cold.
Serving suggestions: green tagliatelle or white bread and mangetout.
Recommended drink: a light red wine.

MINCED BEEF ROLL

SERVES 10–12 ■■
Combination microwave oven
Preparation and cooking time: 1 hour 10 minutes
Kcal per serving if serving 12: 470
P = 32g, F = 30g, C = 19g

2 bread rolls
2 onions
2 garlic cloves
150g/5½oz Parma ham, thinly sliced
500g/1lb 2oz frozen puff pastry
1.25kgs/2¾lbs mixed minced meat
1 tsp chopped fresh oregano
1 tbsp chopped fresh basil
2 eggs
3 egg yolks
salt
freshly ground black pepper
1 tbsp herb mustard
8 x baby Mozzarella cheeses (about 200g/7oz)

1. Place the rolls in a bowl, cover with cold water and set aside to soak. Peel and chop the onions and garlic. Reserve 8 slices of the ham and chop the remainder or purée in a food processor.
2. Arrange the puff pastry sheets side by side in the microwave and thaw on *LOW for 2–3 minutes.*
3. Place the meat in a bowl. Squeeze the water from the rolls. Mix together the meat, rolls, onions, garlic, chopped ham, oregano and basil. Add the eggs and 2 egg yolks, and work to a smooth mixture. Season with salt, pepper and mustard.
4. Dampen the dough sheets, place them next to each other, slightly overlapping, and roll to a rectangle 30 x 40cm/12 x 15 inches.
5. Shape the meat mixture into a long roll and place on the dough. Make a trough along the centre of the meat roll, and line it first with ham slices and then with the

Using a food processor makes a really smooth meat mixture.

Mozzarella cheeses. Wrap the ham around the cheese, and then cover with the meat dough.
6. Wrap the dough around the meat roll, and press the edges together firmly. Beat the remaining egg yolk. Cut stars or leaves from the pastry trimmings to decorate the roll. Brush the surface with the egg yolk, place the decorations in position, and brush them with the egg yolk.
7. Place the meat roll on the lower shelf and cook on *LOW for 30–35 minutes* in a combination microwave preheated to 220°C/425°F (fan-assisted 200°C/400°F) until golden brown.
For an even tastier meat roll add some chopped tomatoes or peppers to the meat mixture.
Serving suggestions: fresh tomato sauce and salad. If serving the meat roll cold, remoulade sauce and a mixed salad make an ideal accompaniment.
Recommended drink: a light red wine.

PORK CHOPS WITH MANGO SAUCE

SERVES 6 ■
Combination microwave oven
Preparation and cooking time: 30 minutes
Kcal per serving: 310
P = 23g, F = 21g, C = 7g

6 x 150g/5½oz pork chops
salt
freshly ground black pepper
2 tbsps curry powder
2 tbsps grated root ginger
1 large ripe mango
2 tbsps vegetable oil
2 tbsps crème fraîche

1. Pat the chops dry and rub salt, pepper, half the curry powder and half the ginger into the flesh.
2. Peel the mango and cut the flesh away from the stone.
3. Brush a microwave-safe roasting pan with half the oil and arrange the chops side by side. Cook on *LOW for 5–6 minutes* with the grill on.
4. Meanwhile, purée the mango flesh with the crème fraîche using a hand-held blender, and season with salt, pepper and the remaining curry powder and the ginger.
5. Turn the chops over and coat with the fruit purée. Cook on *LOW for a further 5–6 minutes* with the grill on.
Serving suggestion: basmati rice.
Recommended drink: a crisp white wine.

SPARERIBS

SERVES 4 ■
Combination microwave oven
Preparation and cooking time: 40 minutes
Marinate for 1 hour
Kcal per serving: 385
P = 29g, F = 25g, C = 1g

1kg/2¼lbs pork spareribs
2 garlic cloves
2 onions
2 tbsps tomato purée
1 tbsp English mustard
3 tbsps soy sauce
2 tbsps vegetable oil
1 tsp caraway seeds
1 tbsp sweet paprika
pinch cayenne pepper
salt
freshly ground black pepper
250ml/9 fl oz brown ale

1. Wash and dry the ribs and chop into 7–10cm/3–4-inch lengths.
2. Peel and chop the garlic and onions. Mix together the garlic, onions, tomato purée, mustard, soy sauce and oil. Stir in the caraway seeds, paprika and cayenne pepper, and season with salt and pepper. Brush the marinade over the pork ribs and leave for 1 hour.
3. Place the marinated ribs on a grill pan with a drip tray. Cook on *MEDIUM for 10 minutes* in a combination microwave preheated to 220°C/425°F (fan-assisted 200°C/400°F). Turn the ribs over, brush with beer and cook on the same settings for a further 10–15 minutes until crisp and well browned.
4. Remove the ribs, cover and keep warm. Pour the contents of the drip tray into a jug. Pour off any fat. Warm through on *HIGH for 3–4 minutes.*
Serving suggestion: potato salad.
Recommended drink: light ale or a red country wine.

LOIN OF LAMB WITH AN OLIVE CRUST

SERVES 4 ■■
Combination microwave oven
Preparation and cooking time: 40 minutes
Kcal per serving: 900
P = 33g, F = 81g, C = 4g

1.25kgs/2¾lbs loin of lamb
salt
freshly ground black pepper
10 black olives, stoned
2 garlic cloves
½ tsp chopped fresh thyme
¼ tsp chopped fresh rosemary
¼ tsp chopped fresh sage
1 tbsp French mustard
2 tbsps breadcrumbs
2–3 tbsps olive oil
125ml/4 fl oz dry red wine
40g/1½oz chilled butter

1. Cut two slits in the skin and fat on either side of the backbone. Rinse the lamb and pat dry. Rub salt and pepper into the flesh.
2. Chop the olives. Peel and finely chop the garlic. Mix together the olives, garlic, thyme, rosemary, sage, mustard and breadcrumbs. Add sufficient oil to make a workable paste.
3. Place the lamb on an ovenproof, microwave-safe dish and spread with the olive and herb paste. Cook on *MEDIUM for 16–20 minutes* in a combination microwave preheated to 220°C/425°F (fan-assisted 200°C/400°F) until golden brown. The cooking time depends on whether the meat is to be rare, medium or well-done. Use a meat thermometer to check the internal temperature.
4. Remove the lamb, wrap in aluminium foil and leave to stand. Pour the wine into the meat juices and reduce on *HIGH for 4–5 minutes*. Dice the butter and beat into the sauce.

Spread the herb paste evenly over the loin.

Dice the chilled butter and beat it into the sauce.

5. Detach the meat from the bone and cut into slices. Serve the sauce separately. The meat continues to cook in the foil, so it is advisable to remove the joint from the oven just before it has reached the required temperature.
Serving suggestions: dauphinois potatoes and grilled tomatoes.
Recommended drink: a dry rosé wine.

SHOULDER OF LAMB COOKED IN A CLAY POT

SERVES 4 ■
Standard microwave oven
Preparation and cooking time: 1 hour
Kcal per serving: 415
P = 44g, F = 20g, C = 10g

1 boneless shoulder of lamb
salt
freshly ground black pepper
3–4 garlic cloves
1 onion
2 yellow peppers
1 red pepper
1 fresh chilli
4 beefsteak tomatoes
5 tbsps olive oil
1 tsp chopped fresh thyme
125ml/4 fl oz dry white wine
1 tbsp chopped fresh parsley

1. Soak the clay pot in cold water.
2. Rinse the lamb and pat dry. Rub salt and pepper into the flesh. Peel the garlic cloves, cut them into long slivers and stud the meat.

> **TIP**
> *Sliced potatoes may also be added to the pepper and tomato mixture.*

3. Peel the onion and cut into matchstick strips. Halve, seed and wash the peppers and chilli and cut into strips.
4. Score the tomato skins, dip in water and cook, covered, at *HIGH for 3–4 minutes*. Rinse in cold water, skin, seed and chop.
5. Place the vegetables in the clay pot, pour over the oil and season with thyme, salt and pepper. Place the lamb joint on top and pour over the wine. Cover and cook on *HIGH for 20 minutes*. Turn the lamb over and cook on the same settings for a further 20–25 minutes.

Stud the shoulder of lamb with slivers of garlic.

Cook the lamb in the microwave on a bed of vegetables.

6. Remove the meat, cover and leave to stand for a few minutes. Cut into slices and serve on the vegetables. Garnish with the parsley.
Serving suggestion: white bread.
Recommended drink: a Greek red country wine.

Lean Cuisine

Stay slim by eating meat – for many there could scarcely be a better way of dieting. Forget those meagre, unsatisfying snacks! Enjoy your food, but keep that extra weight at bay. The recipes in this section use lean cuts of beef, veal, lamb and pork, but fat is kept to a minimum, and seasoning and herbs help to keep an acceptable calorie balance. As a rule, rich breadcrumb coatings, an excess of fat for frying and creamy sauces have been avoided; meat is boiled, braised or grilled. If frying is essential for colour or texture, then a non-stick frying pan is recommended so that the need for oil and fat is limited – the ideal solution for all those who want to cut back on calories, but not on spiciness and flavour.

Beef with Radicchio and Tomatoes (recipe page 112)

BEEF ROULADE WITH VEGETABLE FILLING

SERVES 6 ■■

Preparation and cooking time: 2½ hours
Kcal per serving: 245
P = 34g, F = 6g, C = 5g

1 large carrot
100g/4oz French beans
2 sticks celery
1 small red pepper
salt
freshly ground white pepper
1 x 700g/1lb 10oz topside of beef, thinly sliced
200g/7oz finely minced veal or sausagemeat
2 tbsps grated Parmesan cheese
1 garlic clove
1 tbsp chopped fresh parsley
¼ tsp chopped fresh thyme
2 sage leaves, chopped
2 tbsps olive oil
250ml/9 fl oz full-bodied red wine

Spread the vegetable filling onto the flattened slices of topside.

Roll up the roulades and secure with trussing thread.

1. Peel and dice the carrots. Trim and dice the beans and celery. Halve, seed, wash and dice the pepper. Blanch the carrot, beans, celery and pepper in lightly salted boiling water for 2 minutes. Plunge them straight into ice-cold water and drain.
2. Pat the beef dry and pound with a steak hammer until the slices are half as thick but retain their shape. Rub a little salt and pepper into both sides.
3. Mix together the minced veal or sausagemeat and Parmesan cheese. Peel and finely chop the garlic. Add the parsley, thyme, sage and garlic to the veal or sausagemeat mixture, stir well and season with salt and pepper.
4. Add the carrot, beans, pepper and celery to the filling, and divide between the beef slices, spreading it evenly. Roll up from the narrow sides and secure with trussing thread.

5. Heat the oil in a roasting tin, and fry the roulades until well-browned all over. Add the wine, bring to the boil, cover and simmer for 2 hours, turning the roulades over occasionally. If necessary, add a little water.
6. Remove the roulades from the pan, cover and leave to stand. If required, reduce the sauce a little. Arrange the roulades on a serving dish, and pour over the sauce.
Serving suggestions: white bread and grilled tomatoes.

BOILED SIRLOIN WITH VEGETABLES

SERVES 4 ■■

Preparation and cooking time: 1½ hours
Kcal per serving: 235
P = 26g, F = 12g, C = 6g

3 carrots
½ celery head
1 onion
½ lemon
1.5l/2½ pints water
2 bay leaves
1 thyme sprig
500g/1lb 2oz sirloin
salt
freshly ground black pepper
1 small leek
30g/1oz butter
juice of ½ lemon
3 tbsps snipped chives

1. Peel the carrots and chop 1 of them. Trim and wash the celery and finely chop 1 stick. Peel and halve the onion. Slice the lemon. Place the chopped carrot and celery, the onion, lemon, water, bay leaves and thyme in a flameproof casserole and bring to the boil.

Trim and peel the washed vegetables and then cut them into matchstick strips.

Cook the vegetables in the melted butter and stock until tender but still firm.

> ## TIP
>
> *The quality of the sirloin is an important factor in the success of this dish. If a good sirloin is not available, use the middle section of a beef fillet. Reduce the cooking time by 20 minutes.*

2. Rinse the sirloin and pat dry. Season with salt and pepper.
3. Season the stock with salt, add the sirloin, cover and simmer for 30 minutes. The flesh should remain pink in the middle.
4. Meanwhile, cut the remaining carrots and celery into matchstick strips. Trim and wash the leek and cut into matchstick strips.
5. Melt the butter in a non-stick frying pan, and gently fry the carrots, celery and leek. Season with salt and pepper, and sprinkle with lemon juice. Add 250ml/9 fl oz of the cooking liquid from the meat. Cook the vegetables for 5–7 minutes until tender but still firm.
6. Meanwhile, remove the meat from the pan, cover and leave to stand for a few minutes. Slice the meat thinly and arrange on a dish with the vegetables. Sprinkle with chives and serve.
Serving suggestion: boiled potatoes.

BEEF WITH RADICCHIO AND TOMATOES

(photograph page 108)

SERVES 4 ■
*Preparation and cooking time: 30 minutes
Kcal per serving: 280
P = 27g, F = 18g, C = 3g*

500g/1lb 2oz beef fillet
1–2 garlic cloves
salt
freshly ground black pepper
1 radicchio
1 onion
4 small beefsteak tomatoes
2 tbsps olive oil
1 tbsp lemon juice
6–8 basil leaves, chopped

1. Rinse the beef and pat dry. Cut it into 1cm/½-inch strips. Peel and crush the garlic. Season the beef with salt, pepper and garlic.
2. Wash, trim and shred the radicchio. Peel and chop the onion. Blanch skin, seed and chop the tomatoes.
3. Heat the oil in a non-stick frying pan, and fry the beef strips until well browned. Remove from the pan and keep warm.
4. Gently fry the onion and radicchio in the same pan over a medium heat. Add the tomatoes, sprinkle over the lemon juice, cover and simmer for 3–4 minutes.
5. Return the meat to the pan, and warm through, stirring occasionally. Season with pepper and garnish with chopped basil leaves.
Serving suggestions: white bread.

FILLET STEAKS WITH RED WINE AND ONIONS

SERVES 2 ■
*Preparation and cooking time: 30 minutes
Kcal per serving: 320
P = 38g, F = 13g, C = 3g*

2 small onions
125ml/4 fl oz full-bodied red wine
1 tsp balsamic or red wine vinegar
salt
freshly ground black pepper
2 x 175g/6oz fillet steaks
2 tbsps vegetable oil

1. Peel and finely chop the onions. Place in a small saucepan with the wine and vinegar. Bring to the boil, and continue to boil until the liquid has evaporated. Season with salt and pepper and set aside to cool.
2. Pat the steaks dry and rub pepper into the flesh. Heat the oil in a non-stick frying pan, and fry the steaks over a medium heat for 2–4 minutes on each side, depending on whether you prefer steak rare or well-done.
3. Remove the steaks, season with salt and keep warm. Add the red wine onions to the pan juices, warm through and spoon onto the steaks.
Red wine onions can also be served with roast cutlets.
Serving suggestion: boiled potatoes and a salad of mixed leaves.

RUSSIAN-STYLE RUMP STEAKS

SERVES 2 ■
*Preparation and cooking time: 20 minutes
Kcal per serving: 320
P = 32g, F = 21g, C = 1g*

2 x 150g/5½oz rump steaks
salt
freshly ground black pepper
1 tbsp oil
1 shallot
1 gherkin
1 tbsp Dijon mustard
1 tsp freshly grated horseradish

1. Make a few cuts in the fat on each steak. Pat dry and sprinkle with pepper.
2. Heat the oil in a non-stick frying pan, and fry the steaks over a high heat for 1 minute on each side. Lower the heat, and fry each side for 2–4 minutes, depending on whether you prefer steak rare or well-done.
3. Meanwhile, peel and finely chop the shallot. Finely chop the gherkin. Mix together the shallot, gherkin and mustard.
4. Remove the steaks from the pan, season with salt and coat with the mustard mixture and a sprinkling of grated horseradish. Serve immediately.
Serving suggestion: mashed potato and beetroot.

| **TIP** |
| *Rump steaks are taken from the sirloin and are about 2–3cm/1 inch thick; they usually have a fatty strip on one side.* |

BURGERS WITH BRAISED TOMATOES

SERVES 4 ■
*Preparation and cooking time: 30 minutes
Kcal per serving: 220
P = 31g, F = 9g, C = 4g*

1 onion
500g/1lb 2oz lean minced beef
100g/4oz quark
salt
freshly ground black pepper
1 tsp herb mustard
4 beefsteak tomatoes
1–2 garlic cloves, crushed
2 tbsps olive oil
1 tbsp chopped, fresh oregano or 1 tsp dried oregano
1 tbsp chopped fresh parsley

1. Peel and finely chop the onion. Knead together the minced beef, quark and onion to make a workable mixture. Season well with salt, pepper and mustard, and shape into 4 large, flat burgers.
2. Blanch, skin, quarter and seed the tomatoes. Peel and crush the garlic.
3. Heat the oil in a non-stick frying pan, and fry the burgers over a medium heat for 2 minutes on each side. Arrange the tomatoes around the burgers, add the garlic and sprinkle with oregano. Cover and simmer for 4–5 minutes.
4. Transfer the burgers to a warm serving dish. Top with the tomatoes and sprinkle with parsley.
To add a little extra flavour, top each burger with a slice of Mozzarella cheese for the last few minutes.
Serving suggestion: chips.

BURGERS WITH PEPPER SAUCE

SERVES 4 ■
*Preparation and cooking
time: 40 minutes
Kcal per serving: 385
P = 33g, F = 24g, C = 8g*

*100g/4oz lean, raw ham
400g/14oz minced beef
1 onion
1–2 garlic cloves
1 egg
1 tbsp quark
salt
freshly ground black pepper
1 tsp sweet paprika
pinch cayenne pepper*

FOR THE PEPPER SAUCE:
*1 onion
1 yellow pepper
1 red pepper
2 beefsteak tomatoes
2 tbsps vegetable oil
125ml/4 fl oz meat stock
salt
freshly ground black pepper
pinch sweet paprika
pinch cayenne pepper
1 tbsp chopped parsley*

Chop the ham in a food
processor. Mix with the other
ingredients and knead.

Gently fry the onion and peppers
in the meat juices, season well
and then simmer in the stock.

1. Chop the ham and mix
with the minced beef. Peel
and chop the onion and garlic. Mix together the onion,
garlic, egg and quark, and
add to the meat mixture.
Knead to make a smooth
mixture, and season with
salt, pepper, paprika and
cayenne pepper. Shape the
meat into four burgers.
2. To make the pepper
sauce, peel and chop the
onion. Halve, seed, wash
and dice the peppers.
Blanch, skin, seed and chop
the tomatoes.
3. Heat the oil in a non-stick
frying pan, and fry the burgers for 3–4 minutes on each
side. Remove from the pan
and keep warm.
4. Stir-fry the onion and peppers in the same pan. Add
the tomatoes and stock, and
season with salt, pepper,
paprika and cayenne pep-
per. Stir thoroughly, cover
and simmer for 15 minutes.

5. Place the burgers in the
sauce and heat through for
about 3 minutes. Serve garnished with parsley.
Serving suggestion: boiled
potatoes or green tagliatelle.

MEATLOAF WITH HERBS

SERVES 4 ■
*Preparation and cooking
time: 1 hour 10 minutes
Kcal per serving: 415
P = 37g, F = 27g, C = 6g*

*1 thick slice white bread
100g/4oz raw lean ham
500g/1lb 2oz minced beef
1 egg
1 onion
1 large carrot
3 tbsps chopped fresh parsley
1 tsp chopped fresh
    marjoram
2 chopped sage leaves
1 tsp chopped fresh thyme
grated peel of 1 lemon
1 tsp herb mustard
salt
freshly ground black pepper
20g/¾oz butter
125ml/4 fl oz meat stock
2 beefsteak tomatoes*

Combine the ham and minced
beef. Chop the onion finely and
grate the carrot.

Shape all the ingredients into a
meatloaf. Place in a well-greased
casserole.

1. Place the bread in a bowl,
cover with water and set
aside to soak. Finely chop
the ham in a food processor.
Mix together the ham and
minced beef. Squeeze out
the water from the bread.
Combine the bread with the
meat mixture, add the egg
and stir well.
2. Peel and chop the onion.
Peel and finely grate the carrot. Add the onion, carrot, 2
tbsps of the parsley, the marjoram, sage, thyme and
lemon peel to the meat mixture. Knead thoroughly to
form a smooth mixture, and
season with mustard, salt
and pepper. Shape into a
long meatloaf.
3. Grease an oval casserole
with half the butter, and dice
the remaining butter. Place
the meatloaf in the casserole
and dot with butter. Bake in
a preheated oven at
200°C/400°F/Gas Mark 6
for 15 minutes. Add the
stock, and return to the oven
for a further 15–25 minutes.
4. Blanch, skin, seed and
chop the tomatoes.

5. Remove the meatloaf
from the casserole. Add the
tomatoes to the casserole
and warm through over a
medium heat. Stir in the
remaining parsley.
6. Cut the meatloaf into
slices and arrange on a warm
serving dish. Hand the sauce
separately.
This meatloaf also tastes delicious cold.
Serving suggestion: mashed
potato and Brussels sprouts
or a mixed salad.

HUNGARIAN VEAL GOULASH

SERVES 4
Preparation and cooking time: 1 hour
Kcal per serving: 235
P = 27g, F = 11g, C = 6g

2 small red peppers
250g/8oz onions
50g/2oz lean raw ham
2 tbsps vegetable oil
400g/14oz boneless veal, diced
salt
freshly ground black pepper
1 tbsp sweet paprika
1 tsp chopped fresh marjoram
500ml/18 fl oz meat stock
2 tbsps soured cream
1 tbsp chopped fresh parsley

1. Halve, seed, wash and chop the peppers. Peel and chop the onions. Chop the ham.
2. Heat the oil in a flame-proof casserole, and fry the onions, peppers and ham for 5 minutes over a medium heat.
3. Add the veal, and season with salt, pepper, paprika and marjoram. Mix thoroughly and fry for a further 5 minutes, stirring occasionally. Add the stock, cover and simmer for 30 minutes.
4. Stir in the soured cream, heat through and garnish the goulash with parsley.
Serving suggestions: boiled potatoes or noodles and a green salad.

TIP

The addition of a diced potato will give the goulash sauce a thicker, floury consistency.

ROAST VEAL WITH ROSEMARY

SERVES 4
Preparation and cooking time: 2 hours
Kcal per serving: 235
P = 30g, F = 9g, C = 5g

500g/1lb 2oz topside of veal
2 garlic cloves
salt
freshly ground black pepper
2 sprigs fresh rosemary
50g/2oz Parma ham, thinly sliced
1 onion
2 sticks celery
4 beefsteak tomatoes
1 tbsp olive oil
125ml/4 fl oz dry white wine
2 tbsps chopped fresh parsley

1. Wash the veal and pat dry. Peel and crush the garlic. Rub the veal with salt, pepper and garlic. Lay the rosemary on the joint and cover with overlapping slices of ham. Secure them with trussing thread.
2. Peel and dice the onion. Trim, wash and dice the celery. Blanch, skin, seed and chop the tomatoes.
3. Heat the oil in a roasting tin, and fry the meat until browned all over. Add the onion and celery, and gently fry for a further 5 minutes. Add the tomatoes and wine, and bring to the boil.
4. Cover and cook in a preheated oven at 200°C/400°F/Gas Mark 6 for 45 minutes. Baste the joint with the cooking juices from time to time. Remove the lid and continue to cook for a further 15 minutes.
5. Remove the meat, wrap in aluminium foil and leave to stand for a few minutes. Warm the sauce over a low heat, and stir in the parsley.
6. Cut the veal into slices and arrange on a warm serving dish. Hand the sauce separately.

Rub salt, pepper and garlic into the veal.

Arrange the rosemary sprigs on the meat.

Wrap slices of ham around the meat and secure them with trussing thread.

Serving suggestions: penne or potato gnocchi and a mixed salad.

FILLET OF VEAL WITH CARAMELISED ONIONS

SERVES 2
Preparation and cooking time: 30 minutes
Kcal per serving: 295
P = 32g, F = 7g, C = 13g

6 onions
1 tbsp vegetable oil
1 tsp sugar
300g/10oz fillet of veal
salt
freshly ground white pepper
125ml/4 fl oz rosé wine

1. Peel and quarter the onions. Heat the oil in a non-stick frying pan, and gently fry the onions over a medium heat for a few minutes.
2. Sprinkle sugar over the onions and stir well. Cook until the sugar begins to caramelise.
3. Rinse the veal and pat dry. Rub salt and pepper into the flesh.
4. Push the onions to the edge of the frying pan, add the veal and fry until browned all over.
5. Add the wine, cover and cook for 6–8 minutes, stirring occasionally.
Serving suggestion: crusty white bread.

VEAL ROULADES WITH SAUSAGEMEAT FILLING

SERVES 4 ■
Preparation and cooking time: 1 hour 10 minutes
Kcal per serving: 310
P = 44g, F = 8g, C = 9g

100g/4oz fresh, shelled peas
salt
freshly ground white pepper
150g/5½oz veal sausagemeat
50g/2oz quark
2 tbsps chopped fresh mixed
  herbs
pinch grated nutmeg
grated peel of ½ lemon
4 x 150g/5½oz long, thin veal
  escalopes
1 small onion
1 carrot
1 stick celery
1 tbsp oil
15g/½oz butter
125ml/4 fl oz dry white wine
125ml/4 fl oz veal stock

1. Blanch the peas in lightly salted boiling water, plunge in ice-cold water and set aside to drain.
2. Mix together the sausagemeat and quark. Stir in the herbs and peas, and season with nutmeg, lemon peel, salt and pepper.

> **TIP**
>
> *Instead of veal sausagemeat, try pork sausagemeat. The filling will be tastier although higher in calories.*

3. Pat the veal dry, and flatten carefully with a steak hammer. Rub salt and pepper into the flesh, and coat each escalope with a layer of the sausagemeat mixture. Roll up the escalopes, starting from the long side, and

Roll up the escalopes, starting from the long side, and secure with cocktail sticks or trussing thread.

Fry the roulades with the chopped vegetables. Add the wine and stock, and cook for 30 minutes.

secure with cocktail sticks or trussing thread.
4. Peel and chop the onion and carrot. Trim, wash and chop the celery.
5. Heat the oil and butter in a flameproof casserole, and fry the veal roulades until browned all over. Add the onion, carrot and celery, and fry for a further 5 minutes. Pour in the wine and stock, cover and simmer for 30 minutes.
6. Remove the roulades from the casserole and keep warm. Rub the sauce through a sieve, return to the casserole and allow to reduce a little over a high heat. Pour over the veal roulades and serve.
Serving suggestions: green tagliatelle and carrots.

ROMAN-STYLE VEAL ROULADES

SERVES 4 ■
Preparation and cooking time: 20 minutes
Kcal per serving: 290
P = 32g, F = 16g, C = 2g

8 x 70g/3oz veal escalopes
salt
freshly ground black pepper
50g/2oz Parma ham
1 tsp finely chopped fresh
  sage
2 tbsps oil
4 tbsps Marsala
4 tbsps veal stock
20g/¾oz chilled butter

1. Pat the escalopes dry, and flatten carefully with a steak hammer. Season with salt and pepper.
2. Chop the ham, and mix with the sage. Divide the ham mixture between the escalopes. Roll up the escalopes, starting from the long side, and secure the ends with cocktail sticks.
3. Heat the oil in a non-stick frying pan, and fry the roulades until browned all over. Add the Marsala and stock. Cover and cook for 2–3 minutes.
4. Remove the roulades from the pan and keep warm. Bring the sauce to the boil over a high heat and allow to reduce slightly.
5. Dice the butter, and beat into the sauce, a few pieces at a time. Pour the sauce over the roulades and serve.
Serving suggestions: white bread and petits pois.

VEAL CUTLETS WITH SPRING ONIONS

SERVES 2 ■
Preparation and cooking time: 25 minutes
Kcal per serving: 270
P = 33g, F = 10g, C = 3g

2 x 200g/7oz veal cutlets
1 garlic clove
½ tsp dried thyme
salt
freshly ground white pepper
bunch of small spring onions
1 tbsp oil
100ml/3 fl oz white wine
1 tbsp balsamic or white
  wine vinegar

1. Pat the cutlets dry. Peel and crush the garlic. Rub the cutlets with the garlic, thyme, salt and pepper.
2. Trim, wash and chop the spring onions.
3. Heat the oil in a non-stick frying pan, and fry the cutlets over a medium heat for 2 minutes on each side. Remove the meat, and fry the spring onions in the same pan. Add the wine and vinegar, return the cutlets to the pan, cover and cook for 8–10 minutes.
4. Arrange the veal on warmed plates and top with the spring onions. If necessary, reduce the sauce a little and then pour over the onions.
Serving suggestion: white bread.

> **TIP**
>
> *Try spring onions cooked in this way with lamb cutlets.*

SWEET AND SOUR PORK

SERVES 4
Preparation and cooking time: 40 minutes
Kcal per serving: 395
P = 20g, F = 24g, C = 14g

400g/14oz pork fillet
1 tsp cornflour
2 tbsps soy sauce
1 tbsp sherry vinegar
6 tbsps rice wine or dry
    sherry
1 tsp tomato purée
1 tsp freshly grated
    horseradish
pinch cayenne pepper
½ pineapple
1 small leek
1 small red pepper
1 small yellow pepper
1 chilli
3 tbsps groundnut oil
salt
freshly ground black pepper

1. Rinse the pork and pat dry. Trim, if necessary, and cut into slices.
2. Mix together the cornflour, soy sauce, vinegar, rice wine or sherry, tomato purée and horseradish in a shallow dish. Season the pork with cayenne pepper and place in the marinade. Set aside for 15 minutes.

> ### TIP
> *This is a low-calorie but still very tasty variation of a traditional Chinese recipe, in which the meat is first dipped in batter, then fried in hot oil and finally dipped in a vegetable sauce.*

3. Meanwhile, peel, core and dice the pineapple. Trim, wash and slice the leek.

Mix the meat, pineapple and the reserved marinade with the fried vegetables and warm through.

Halve, seed, wash and dice the peppers. Halve, seed wash and finely chop the chilli.
4. Heat 2 tbsps of the oil in a wok or frying pan, and stir-fry the leek, peppers and chilli over a medium heat for 5–6 minutes.
5. Heat the remaining oil in a non-stick frying pan. Drain the pork and reserve the marinade. Fry the pork over a high heat until browned on both sides.
6. Mix the meat, pineapple and the reserved marinade with the fried vegetables and heat through over a high heat for 2–3 minutes.
7. Season with salt and pepper and serve immediately.
Serving suggestion: fluffy boiled rice.

PORK WITH CHINESE CABBAGE

SERVES 2
Preparation and cooking time: 30 minutes
Kcal per serving: 325
P = 24g, F = 25g, C = 1g

1 x 200g/7oz Chinese
    cabbage
250g/8oz pork fillet
2 tbsps sesame oil
salt
freshly ground white pepper
1 tsp grated root ginger
1 tsp mild curry powder
2 tbsps soy sauce
1 tsp finely chopped fresh
    coriander leaves

1. Discard any wilted outer leaves from the Chinese cabbage and cut it in half. Remove the tough stalk and shred the leaves.
2. Rinse the pork and pat dry. Trim, if necessary, and slice thinly.
3. Heat the oil in a wok or frying pan. Stir-fry the cabbage for 3–5 minutes. Add the pork, and stir-fry until browned all over.
4. Season with salt and pepper, and add the ginger, curry powder and soy sauce. Sprinkle over the chopped coriander and serve immediately.
If Chinese cabbage is not available, use white cabbage.
Serving suggestion: fluffy, boiled rice.

MEAT AND VEGETABLE KEBABS

SERVES 4
Preparation and cooking time: 40 minutes
Marinate for 2 hours
Kcal per serving: 285
P = 21g, F = 17g, C = 5g

400g/14oz pork fillet
2 small courgettes
1 red pepper
1 yellow pepper
2 onions

FOR THE MARINADE:
2 tbsps vegetable oil
2 tbsps soy sauce
3 tbsps dry sherry
1 tbsp tomato purée
pinch grated root ginger
½ tsp 5-spice powder
freshly ground black pepper

1. Rinse the pork and pat dry. Rinse, trim and cut the courgettes into 1cm/½-inch slices. Halve, seed and wash the peppers. Cut into 3cm/1-inch squares. Peel and quarter the onions. Thread alternate cubes of meat and vegetables on to 4 kebab skewers.
2. Thoroughly mix together all the ingredients for the marinade. Brush the marinade over the kebabs, cover and set aside for 2 hours.
3. Place the kebabs under a preheated grill or on a barbecue, and cook for 5–7 minutes. Brush the kebabs frequently with the remaining marinade.
Serving suggestion: potatoes baked in foil.

> ### TIP
> *Place a sheet of aluminium foil under the grill pan.*

LAMB RAGOÛT WITH ARTICHOKES AND LEMON SAUCE

SERVES 4 ■ ■

*Preparation and cooking
time: 45 minutes
Kcal per serving: 475
P = 31g, F = 31g, C = 18g*

8 small, young globe
  artichokes
juice of 1 lemon
500g/1lb 2oz boneless leg of
  lamb
salt
freshly ground black pepper
2 shallots
1 garlic clove
2 tbsps vegetable oil
125ml/4 fl oz veal stock

FOR THE LEMON SAUCE:
2 eggs, separated
salt
juice of 1 lemon
1 tbsp chopped fresh parsley

*Cut off the lower artichoke leaves
and the tips of the upper leaves.
Halve and remove the chokes.*

*Fry the meat and artichokes, pour
in the stock and simmer for 30
minutes.*

*Fold the whisked egg white
mixture into the ragoût and warm
through.*

1. Break off the artichoke stalks and brush with lemon juice to prevent discolouration. Cut off the lower leaves and tips of the upper leaves. Halve the artichokes, discard the chokes and place the halves in a bowl of water with the remaining lemon juice.

2. Rinse the lamb and pat dry. Cut into 3cm/1-inch cubes, and season with salt and pepper.

3. Peel and chop the shallots and garlic. Heat the oil, and fry the shallots and garlic until transparent.

4. Add the lamb and artichokes, and fry for 5 minutes, stirring frequently. Pour in the stock, cover and simmer for about 30 minutes.

5. To make the lemon sauce, whisk the egg whites with a pinch of salt until they form stiff peaks. Slowly add the lemon juice, egg yolks and parsley. Fold the mixture into the ragoût, warm through quickly but do not allow to boil. As an alternative, use veal instead of lamb.

Serving suggestion: tagliatelle or boiled potatoes.

BOILED SHOULDER OF LAMB ON A BED OF VEGETABLES

SERVES 4 ■

*Preparation and cooking
time: 1 hour 40 minutes
Kcal per serving: 630
P = 48g, F = 45g, C = 8g*

1kg/2¼lbs boneless shoulder
  of lamb
2 garlic cloves
salt
freshly ground black pepper
1 onion
5 peppercorns
2 bay leaves
2 thyme sprigs
1 rosemary sprig
2 sage leaves
1 bouquet garni
1l/1¾ pints water
2 tbsps balsamic or white
  wine vinegar
4 carrots
1 kohlrabi
200g/7oz tender French
  beans
1 tbsp chopped fresh parsley

1. Rinse the lamb and pat dry. Peel and crush the garlic. Rub salt, pepper and garlic into the meat.

> **TIP**
>
> *The smaller and succulent fore knuckles can be cooked in this way. The choice of vegetables may vary according to the season.*

2. Peel and quarter the onion. Place the onion, peppercorns, bay leaves, thyme, rosemary, sage and bouquet garni in a flameproof casserole. Add the water and vinegar and bring to the boil. Add the lamb, cover and simmer for 1¼ hours.

3. Meanwhile, peel and slice the carrots. Peel the kohlrabi

Peel and crush the garlic.

*Wash the sage and combine with
the other herbs.*

and cut into matchstick strips. Trim the French beans and, if necessary, remove any strings.

4. Remove the cooked lamb from the liquid, wrap in aluminium foil and leave to stand.

5. Rub the cooking liquid through a sieve, return to the casserole and bring to the boil. Add the carrots and kohlrabi, and cook for about 5 minutes. Add the beans, and cook until tender but still firm. Remove the vegetables with a slotted spoon and place them in a deep serving dish. Bring the cooking liquid back to the boil and allow to reduce slightly.

6. Cut the lamb into thin slices and arrange them on the vegetables. Pour over the sauce and garnish with chopped parsley.

Serving suggestion: boiled potatoes.

Index